Written by **A.R.A**

# Work-Life Balance:

## Thrive as a Remote Worker

Copyright © 2024 A.R.A . All rights reserved.

No part of this publication may be reproduced, distributed, or transmitted in any form or by any means, including photocopying, recording, or other electronic or mechanical methods, without the prior written permission of the publisher, except in the case of brief quotations embodied in critical reviews and certain other non-commercial uses permitted by copyright law.

For permission requests, write to the publisher, addressed "Attention: Permissions Coordinator," at the email below:

archyspectar123@gmail.com

# TABLE OF CONTENT

PREFACE ................................................................ 6

   Understanding Work-Life Balance ...................... 11

   The Challenges of Remote Work ......................... 21

   Setting Boundaries: Work Stays at Work ............. 37

   Designing the Perfect Home Office .................... 47

   The Power of a Morning Routine ........................ 57

   Creating a Daily Schedule That Works ............... 66

   Effective Time Blocking for Remote Workers ..... 76

   Managing Distractions and Staying Focused ........ 88

   Dealing with Family and Household Interruptions ................................................................................. 98

   Lunch Break and Downtime: Why You Need Them ................................................................................ 112

   Mastering Communication with Remote Teams 122

   The Role of Technology in Achieving Balance .. 135

   Managing Your Energy, Not Just Your Time .... 149

   The Importance of Flexibility ............................. 166

Burnout Prevention for Remote Workers .......... **184**

Creating a Work-Life Integration Strategy ......... **195**

The Importance of Saying No ........................... **207**

Mental Health and Self-Care in Remote Work ... **216**

Staying Connected: Maintaining Relationships in Remote Work ..................................................... **227**

Reviewing and Adjusting Your Routine ............. **236**

CONCLUSION ..................................................... **245**

# PREFACE

Welcome to the age of remote work, a phenomenon that has altered not just the way we work but also how we live. While remote work was formerly considered a luxury reserved for freelancers and digital nomads, it is now an essential component of many people's professional lives. This transformation occurred quickly, thanks in large part to the COVID-19 epidemic, but the changes are permanent. As we negotiate this new normal, it's critical to investigate the influence of remote work on our daily lives and how we may prosper in this setting.

**The Shift Toward Remote Work**

Remote employment is not new, but it skyrocketed in popularity during the pandemic, when businesses needed to adjust swiftly. Prior to the epidemic, many organizations opposed the notion, fearing a loss of production. Businesses immediately recognized that employees could maintain, if not increase, their performance while working from home. Studies have found that remote workers are more productive and satisfied with their careers than those who operate in regular office environments.

According to a McKinsey analysis from 2022, 58% of Americans reported being able to work remotely at least part-time, with 35% having the ability to work from home full-time. This is a global trend, with organizations in Europe and Asia adopting flexible work structures to meet their employees' demands. These figures demonstrate how remote work has evolved from a temporary solution to a permanent fixture in the global economy.

**Benefits and Challenges of Remote Work**

The advent of remote work delivers a number of advantages, including greater flexibility, autonomy, and the elimination of commute. Employees are able to plan their days in ways that best meet their personal and professional demands. Many people benefit from this flexibility because it helps them to achieve a better work-life balance, which contributes to their overall well-being.

However, remote employment does not come without its problems. The blurring barriers between home and work life might result in longer working hours, higher stress, and a sense of isolation. Many remote workers struggle to "switch off," which contributes to burnout. Furthermore, communication and collaboration might become more complex, necessitating a more deliberate effort to sustain team chemistry.

**Why Work-Life Balance Matters Now More Than Ever**

As we adjust to our new working environment, one thing is clear: attaining work-life balance is more important than ever. In a typical office, physical separation distinguished between work and personal time. However, when your office is your living room or bedroom, these lines become blurred. This booklet will go over ideas for preserving a work-life balance while working remotely.

The following chapters will walk you through practical strategies and advice on creating limits, managing time, and reducing burnout. Whether you're new to remote work or want to better your work-life balance, this guide will help you thrive in this new normal.

In this new era of work, the task is more than just being productive; it is also about achieving balance. Welcome to this trip.

# Understanding Work-Life Balance

In today's digital age, particularly with the advent of remote employment, the concept of work-life balance has become increasingly important. Employees are no longer limited to the typical 9-to-5 office model; rather, the lines between work and personal life have blurred. But what does "work-life balance" include, and why is it so important?

This chapter explores the concept of work-life balance, its impact on personal and professional success, and practical strategies for achieving it.

### Defining Work-Life Balance

Work-life balance is fundamentally about striking a balance between the responsibilities of your career and the needs of your personal life. It's about balancing both without allowing one to overpower the other. Achieving this balance allows you to be productive at work while also having time to relax, pursue hobbies, cultivate relationships, and maintain your physical and mental health.

For many, remote work provides freedom, but it also presents the issue of determining when to stop working. The temptation to check emails after hours or do that "one last task" is relentless, and it can disrupt personal time. As a result, understanding the principles of work-life balance assists remote workers in maintaining boundaries between their professional and personal lives.

### Why Work-Life Balance Matters

Maintaining a proper work-life balance is crucial for multiple reasons:

- Improved Mental Health: Overwork can lead to burnout, anxiety, and depression. Balancing work and personal pursuits minimizes stress and improves mental health.

- Increased Productivity: Contrary to popular assumption, employees who maintain a work-life balance are more efficient and focused at work.

- Better Physical Health: A balanced lifestyle makes time for physical activities like exercise, which can lower the risk of illnesses connected with sedentary lifestyles (such cardiovascular disease or diabetes).

- Stronger Relationships: Whether with family, friends, or partners, taking time away from work to interact with loved ones is critical for maintaining good relationships.

- Career Longevity: Sustainable work practices lower the danger of burnout, allowing you to retain long-term career happiness while also prioritizing your personal well-being.

## Common Misconceptions about Work-Life Balance

Many individuals feel that work-life balance entails equal time spent on work and personal activities. However, this isn't always true. Balance does not always imply spending the same amount of hours on work as on pleasure. It's about making sure that no part of life takes precedence over the others.

For some, attaining balance may include working long hours during certain periods and compensating with more personal time later. Others may find it necessary to strictly adhere to a predetermined schedule in order to keep work inside particular hours. The idea is to find a rhythm that suits your specific requirements and circumstances.

**Signs of Poor Work-Life Balance**

Before delving into solutions, it's critical to identify the symptoms of poor work-life balance:

- Constant Overwork: If you frequently work late at night or on weekends, it may suggest a lack of balance.

- Feeling Overwhelmed: Another indicator is a constant sense of being on the go, with no time to relax or unwind.

- Health Decline: Neglecting sleep, exercise, or good nutrition owing to work demands can indicate an imbalance.

- Strained Relationships: If your professional obligations prevent you from spending quality time with your loved ones, it's time to reevaluate your priorities.

Recognizing these signs is the first step toward achieving meaningful transformation.

**Creating Work-Life Balance: Strategies for Remote Workers**

Because the lines between home and work are blurred, attaining balance can be difficult for remote workers. However, with intentional effort, it is possible to establish clear limits and adopt routines that promote good balance. Here are some practical tactics you can use:

- Establish Clear Work Hours: Follow a set routine as much as possible. This keeps work from leaking into your leisure time and helps you stay organized.

- Create a Dedicated Workspace: Even if you don't have a home office, set aside a specific area for work. This helps to mentally separate work and relaxing areas.

- Prioritize projects: Use time management techniques such as the Eisenhower Matrix or the Pomodoro Technique to focus on high-priority projects during work hours while minimizing wasted time.

- Take Regular Breaks: Taking short breaks away from your work might help you stay productive and prevent mental tiredness.

- Learn to Say No: Know your limits and avoid overcommitting. Recognize when you need to protect your personal time, whether that means taking on extra duties or consenting to too many meetings.

- Use Technology Wisely: Scheduling software, task managers, and even automated "Do Not Disturb" settings can all help you keep work and leisure time separate.

- Practice Self-Care: Make time for activities that promote your well-being, such as exercise, meditation, or indulging in hobbies you enjoy.

## Employers' Role in Promoting Work-Life Balance

While individuals have a large portion of the responsibility for preserving balance, employers play an important role as well. Companies that promote work-life balance not only improve employee well-being, but also raise productivity, reduce absenteeism, and boost job satisfaction.

Employers can promote a healthier work-life balance in several ways, including:

- Flexible working hours enable employees to plan their workday around personal commitments.

- Limiting After-Hours Communication: Fostering an environment in which emails and work communications are not expected after hours.

- Providing Mental Health Support: Offering tools such as therapy or mental health days to help employees cope with their emotions.

**Measuring Your Work/Life Balance**

How do you know whether you've found a nice balance? Regularly check in with yourself. Do you feel worried or relaxed? Do you have adequate time for family, hobbies, and self-care? Are you executing tasks efficiently and without feeling overwhelmed?

It's also a good idea to assess your daily activities on a regular basis and make any necessary improvements. As your professional and personal lives grow, so will your balance methods.

Work-life balance isn't a one-size-fits-all approach. What works for one individual may not work for others. The goal is to develop a regimen that allows you to balance your business duties with your personal demands. Implementing the ideas described in this chapter will better prepare you to negotiate the complexity of remote work and live a satisfying, balanced life.

The following chapters of this booklet will present further tools and approaches to help you maintain this balance, avoid burnout, and eventually thrive as a remote worker.

# The Challenges of Remote Work

The development of remote employment has transformed the landscape of modern careers. For many, it has become a tempting alternative to regular office jobs, offering greater flexibility, reducing daily commutes, and allowing people to work from the comfort of their homes. While there are indisputable benefits to remote work, it also presents a unique set of obstacles that, if not managed appropriately, can have an impact on productivity, job satisfaction, and general well-being.

In this chapter, we will go thoroughly into the primary issues related with remote work and present effective solutions to overcome them. Remote workers can retain good performance and personal satisfaction if they grasp the challenges and use appropriate tactics.

**Blurred Boundaries Between Work and Personal Life**

One of the most difficult aspects of remote work is separating professional and personal time. In typical office settings, the physical act of commuting provides a seamless transition between work and personal life. Remote employment removes this boundaries, allowing professional responsibilities to spill over into personal time.

Why Does This Happen? The lack of a distinct workspace contributes significantly to this blurring of lines. Working from the same area where you rest or sleep, such as a living room or bedroom, might make it difficult to mentally disconnect from work. Furthermore, the flexibility of remote employment might lead to ambiguous limits. Without the set start and end timings of a traditional workweek, employees may find themselves responding to emails or doing activities much after official hours have past.

Impact: The merging of work and personal life can lead to burnout, increased stress, and a breakdown in personal relationships. It becomes difficult to completely disengage from work, resulting in a perpetual sense of being "on call." This can also have an impact on personal well-being because a lack of adequate downtime prevents relaxation and recovery.

Solution: To combat this, it is critical to establish clear boundaries between work and personal time. Designating a different workspace from where you relax can help you maintain a mental distance between the two worlds. Furthermore, setting specific working hours can mark the end of the day and develop a habit that reinforces the boundary between work and personal time. Communication is also important; inform coworkers and superiors of your working hours so that they respect your personal time.

**Feelings of Isolation**

Another key difficulty for remote workers is the sense of isolation. Working alone for an extended amount of time can cause loneliness, especially for people who thrive in social situations. Casual encounters that occur in a regular office setting—whether through water-cooler conversations, impromptu team discussions, or collaborative projects—are frequently absent in a remote work environment.

Why Does This Happen? The remote nature of employment inherently reduces face-to-face interactions, which are essential for developing connections and creating team cohesion. While video conversations and online meetings assist to bridge the gap, they cannot truly capture the depth of in-person interactions. Furthermore, communication in remote work situations is generally transactional, with a focus on task completion rather than social ties. Without these informal encounters, employees may feel estranged from both their coworkers and the overall business culture.

Impact: A lack of social connection might have a harmful effect on mental health. Isolation can eventually lead to lower motivation, engagement, and even a sense of separation from the company's objective. In extreme circumstances, it can cause despair or anxiety, particularly among professionals who rely on social connection for mental well-being.

Solution: To alleviate emotions of loneliness, make regular connections with coworkers. Scheduling non-work-related check-ins allows for more relaxed interactions and helps to preserve relationships. Virtual team-building activities or social events, such as virtual coffee breaks or informal online hangouts, can also serve to recreate the camaraderie of an office setting. Making an effort to engage with coworkers outside of work responsibilities is critical for sustaining a sense of community.

## Communication Breakdowns

Communication is the foundation of any successful remote collaboration, but it also poses one of the most difficult problems. In an office setting, employees can simply ask questions, clarify points, and resolve misunderstandings by stepping over to a colleague's desk. Remote work, on the other hand, is primarily dependent on digital communication methods such as email, chat platforms, and video chats, which are more prone to delays, misinterpretations, and incomplete communications.

Why Does This Happen? Remote communication is frequently asynchronous, which means that a message is transmitted and then received and reacted to after a wait. This lack of immediacy can cause inefficiencies, particularly when urgent choices are required. Written messages are also more prone to misinterpretation because they lack nonverbal clues such as facial expressions or tone of voice. Furthermore, the sheer amount of communication tools—Slack, Zoom, email, and others can overwhelm employees, resulting in missing or overlooked messages.

Impact: Poor communication can result in blunders, missed deadlines, and frustration among team members. When team members are not on the same page, productivity suffers, task confusion arises, and morale plummets. Over time, this can lead to team conflict and a decrease in overall job quality.

Solution: Clear protocols are essential for improving remote communication. Teams should have criteria regarding which tools to utilize in certain situations, such as email for formal communication, chat platforms for fast questions, and video calls for in-depth conversations. Furthermore, it is preferable to err on the side of over-communication, ensuring that responsibilities are clearly defined, expectations are established, and any questions are completely addressed. This decreases the likelihood of misunderstandings and keeps everyone on track.

**Lack of Routine**

The flexibility of remote work is one of its greatest advantages, but it also brings with it the challenge of maintaining a consistent routine. Without the structure of a traditional office environment, some workers find it difficult to manage their time effectively or stay organized. The presence of household distractions, such as chores or family members, can also disrupt focus and productivity.

Why Does This Happen? It's easy to lose track of time when you don't have a regular office routine. Workers at an office have a predetermined schedule, which includes arriving at a specific time, having lunch breaks, and completing responsibilities before leaving. Remote employment lacks this inherent structure, making it difficult for some people to create a routine. Working from home also brings a variety of possible distractions, such as domestic obligations and the temptation to relax.

Impact: A lack of routine can result in missed deadlines, procrastination, and an overall sense of disorder. Workers may feel overwhelmed as they seek to balance their time and duties. This can cause stress and have a detrimental long-term influence on job performance.

Solution: To solve this difficulty, establish a disciplined regimen. Setting a definite start and end time for the workday promotes a sense of accountability. Time-blocking tools, which allocate specific parts of the day to specific tasks, can help you stay focused and avoid procrastinating. Minimizing distractions is also key; this can be accomplished by setting limits with family members, employing equipment such as noise-canceling headphones, and devoting time to home activities outside of work hours.

**Overworking and Burnout**

While the concept of working from home is frequently connected with improved work-life balance, many remote workers report the reverse. The lack of obvious physical boundaries between home and work might lead to overwork. Many remote employees feel compelled to demonstrate their productivity, which can lead to longer hours, fewer breaks, and an increased risk of burnout.

.Why Does This Happen? The freedom of remote work can result in a lack of defined limits. Without the commute, which traditionally marks the end of the workday, remote workers may find themselves working late into the evening. Furthermore, there may be a perceived need to demonstrate productivity to superiors and coworkers, particularly in businesses where remote work is still relatively new. This causes employees to go above and above in order to demonstrate their worth.

Impact: Overworking can have major effects on both mental and physical health. Burnout, defined by feelings of tiredness, detachment, and inefficacy, is a common side effect of chronic overwork. In addition to its impact on personal well-being, burnout can have a detrimental impact on productivity, creativity, and overall job performance. Workers who are burnt out are more likely to get alienated from their roles and may finally leave in quest of a better work-life balance.

Solution: To avoid burnout, set firm work hours and take regular breaks. Setting reminders or alarms to signify the end of the workday can help you establish a habit that separates work and personal time. Taking regular breaks throughout the day, as well as longer pauses for meals or exercise, can also help you recharge and stay focused. Prioritizing self-care and recognizing burnout symptoms early on can help avert harmful consequences.

## Reduced Access to Career Development Opportunities

One of the more subtle disadvantages of remote employment is the limited access to career development opportunities. In typical office settings, employees frequently have informal opportunities to network with coworkers, seek mentorship, and achieve visibility with managers. These chances are less common in remote work environments, which might make some employees feel detached from career progression opportunities.

Why Does This Happen? Remote workers frequently feel "out of sight, out of mind" when it comes to promotions or important initiatives. Without the casual face-to-face encounters that occur in an office, remote workers may struggle to establish their presence and showcase their contributions. Furthermore, remote work environments frequently lack the spontaneous mentorship possibilities that exist in office settings, when senior employees might provide assistance or career advise through casual conversations.

Impact: Remote professionals may feel stuck in their employment if they do not have regular access to opportunities for professional development. This might lead to a drop in motivation as employees feel ignored for promotions or important assignments. Over time, a lack of upward mobility can lead to workplace unhappiness, as employees believe their efforts are not recognized or rewarded. This stasis can also impede long-term career success, as a lack of mentorship and networking limits prospects for skill development and advancement.

Solution: Remote workers must be proactive about their professional growth. Regular one-on-one meetings with managers to discuss career objectives, performance, and professional development can assist remote employees stay visible and linked to growth possibilities. Furthermore, pursuing virtual mentorships, whether within the organization or through external professional networks, can help provide the guidance and feedback required to advance in one's career. Participating in online professional networks, attending virtual conferences, and seeking learning opportunities, such as online courses, can all help remote professionals grow and develop in their professions.

Remote employment offers a new way of approaching our careers, with advantages such as flexibility, comfort, and autonomy. However, these benefits come with unique problems that must be identified and handled in order to create a productive and fulfilling remote work experience. Remote workers must learn skills to overcome the challenges of blurring work-life boundaries, feelings of isolation, and communication breakdowns.

Remote workers can reduce the risks of overworking, burnout, and career stagnation by establishing clear limits, developing disciplined routines, enhancing communication techniques, and promoting personal well-being. Proactively exploring career development opportunities and keeping social interactions with coworkers helps remote workers stay motivated and progress in their professions.

In the following chapters, we will look at more in-depth ideas for creating a sustainable and successful remote work environment. Topics such as setting up a home office to increase productivity, optimizing time management practices, and striking a balance between freedom and discipline will provide the tools needed to prosper in a remote career. Individuals who approach remote work with intentionality and a willingness to adapt can realize the full potential of this modern work style, turning problems into opportunities for growth and success.

# Setting Boundaries: Work Stays at Work

One of the most major issues that remote workers experience is the inability to separate their work and personal lives. Without the clear physical barrier that a traditional office provides, work can easily spill over into personal time, resulting in stress, exhaustion, and a sense of being "always on." As a result, setting hard boundaries is critical for achieving a healthy work-life balance, increasing productivity, and safeguarding mental and physical health. This chapter will explain why setting boundaries is important, offer ways for keeping work and personal life separate, and look at the benefits of properly maintaining these boundaries.

## Why Boundaries Are Crucial for Remote Workers

Setting boundaries separates work and personal life, which is critical for sustaining both mental and physical wellness. When remote workers fail to set these boundaries, they frequently face a series of negative repercussions. For example, a lack of separation between work and home life might result in extended working hours, since people feel obliged to check emails late at night or on weekends. This constant influx of professional responsibilities can lead to feelings of overwhelm, with personal obligations being pushed aside, resulting in anger and resentment. Furthermore, when work consumes more time than it should, personal well-being suffers as self-care activities such as exercise, relaxation, and spending meaningful time with loved ones are overlooked.

The key to avoiding these undesirable results is to learn how to establish and maintain solid boundaries that prevent work from overshadowing personal time. In the following sections, we will go over how to set various types of limits that can help remote workers live a more balanced lifestyle.

## Physical Boundaries: Creating a Defined Workspace

Creating a defined workspace is one of the most simple but effective strategies to divide work and personal life. Even if you don't have a dedicated home office, you can still designate a special location for work. By doing so, you can mentally "clock in" when entering that location and "clock out" while leaving it, indicating a definite beginning and finish to your workday.

When creating a dedicated workstation, try selecting a quiet location that reduces distractions and helps you to concentrate. Also, keep business equipment like your computer and documents away from personal belongings. This physical barrier strengthens mental boundaries, making it simpler to differentiate between work and leisure time. Personalizing your workstation with comfy furniture and inspired decor can make it a more fun place to work while maintaining a professional environment. This contributes to a more structured atmosphere in which work tasks are limited to a certain region.

## Time Boundaries: Establishing Work Hours

While remote work gives flexibility, it also runs the potential of making it difficult to "turn off" work at the end of the day. Without the structure of a regular office environment, many remote workers struggle to distinguish between work and personal time. Setting specific work hours is one of the most important tactics for keeping healthy boundaries.

To define time restrictions, establish consistent working hours and adhere to them as much as feasible. This pattern establishes a sense of normalcy and indicates when work begins and ends. Using alarms or reminders to indicate the beginning and conclusion of your workday can help you stick to this routine and avoid working late into the night. Furthermore, express your working hours to coworkers and managers, encouraging them to respect your boundaries and avoid contacting you outside of these hours unless absolutely essential.

**Digital Boundaries: Managing Technology**

Remote work has become more accessible because to technological advancements, but it is also increasingly difficult to unplug. With frequent notifications from emails, messaging applications, and project management tools, work can easily eat into personal time. As a result, regulating your access to work tools is an essential step in establishing boundaries.

One method for managing digital boundaries is to turn off work-related notifications during your personal time. This eliminates the distraction of constant warnings, allowing you to focus on non-work activities. If possible, utilize distinct devices for work and personal chores, such as a business laptop and a personal phone, to make it easier to detach from work at the end of the day. Additionally, use your devices'"Do Not Disturb" settings to block work notifications during particular hours, ensuring that you have uninterrupted personal time.

**Emotional Boundaries: Protecting Your Personal Time**

Emotional boundaries are also vital for keeping professional stress from affecting your personal life. Remote professionals frequently take the stress of their work tasks into their personal lives, hurting their moods and relationships. Setting emotional boundaries allows you to mentally separate from work and enjoy your leisure time more fully.

Mindfulness is an effective approach to set emotional boundaries. Before switching from business to personal time, take a few moments to halt, breathe, or perhaps go for a short stroll. Stress-relieving activities such as exercise, hobbies, or spending time with loved ones after work can also help you relax and move your attention away from work-related issues. It's also critical to avoid the temptation to focus on professional activities during personal time; teaching yourself to leave work-related thoughts behind at the end of the day can significantly improve your mental health.

## Managing Boundaries with Family and Friends

One of the difficulties of remote work is that family members or roommates may not always recognize the need for limits. They may disrupt your workday or believe that you are available for personal affairs at all times. Communicating your job limits clearly to those around you is critical for staying focused and productive.

Letting family members or housemates know about your job schedule can assist them understand when you're available and when you're not. You can also use signs, such as closing the door or wearing headphones, to indicate that you are in work mode and should not be bothered. While flexibility is crucial, avoid allowing personal needs to frequently interfere with your work time, since this can make it difficult to maintain a clear boundary between work and personal life.

## Handling Boundary Pushers

Despite your best attempts to establish boundaries, certain people—whether coworkers, bosses, or clients—may continue to challenge them. They may send late-night emails or demand you to be available on your personal time. In these instances, it is critical to assertively set your boundaries.

Begin by setting expectations early, informing others about your working hours and personal boundaries. If someone calls you outside of business hours, react gently but firmly, saying that you will handle the request the next weekday. Consistency is essential; responding to after-hours inquiries shows that you're available, encouraging individuals to continue pushing the boundaries.

**The Benefits of Setting Boundaries**

Setting and maintaining clear boundaries as a remote worker has various advantages. First and foremost, it promotes mental health by lowering stress and preventing burnout, allowing you more control over your schedule. Furthermore, clear boundaries allow you to be more productive at work since you can concentrate on responsibilities without being distracted by personal issues. Strong boundaries also improve personal connections by providing you more time and energy to spend with your loved ones, pursue interests, and care for yourself. Finally, setting boundaries ensures long-term professional sustainability by preventing burnout and promoting a healthy work-life balance.

Setting boundaries is critical to success as a remote worker. You can achieve a healthy work-life balance by setting up a separate workstation, sticking to typical work hours, managing digital distractions, and safeguarding your emotional well-being. These limits enable you to remain productive during work hours while also protecting your personal time and well-being, ensuring that work stays at work and your personal life thrives.

# Designing the Perfect Home Office

As remote work becomes the new normal for many, the architecture of a home office has become increasingly important. A well-designed home office can boost productivity, reduce stress, and create a pleasant, professional environment that allows for extended hours of focused work. This chapter will look at the major factors to consider when constructing the ideal home office, including location, ergonomics, lighting, organization, aesthetics, technology, and sound management, all with the purpose of increasing efficiency and well-being.

**Choosing the Right Location for Your Home Office**

The location of your home office is crucial for creating a productive, distraction-free environment. When selecting the ideal location, privacy should be the first concern. If feasible, find a room or corner of your home where you may work uninterrupted. A spare room is great, but a quiet spot away from the main living rooms can do wonders to reduce distractions. Furthermore, being near a window is ideal since it gives natural light, which has been proved to increase mood, energy, and focus. However, avoid direct sunlight, as it can produce glare on your screen.

For those who live in limited areas, inventiveness is essential. Consider installing room separators or transforming unused spaces like closets or nooks into functional workstations. Even in small living quarters, you can create a designated environment that helps you mentally transition into "work mode" each day.

# Prioritizing Ergonomics for Long-Term Comfort

Ergonomics is essential in designing a workspace that promotes your health and comfort, especially if you spend long hours sitting at a desk. The proper ergonomic setup can help you avoid weariness, physical strain, and long-term health issues like back and neck pain. To begin, select a desk that allows your elbows to rest at a 90-degree angle when typing, keeping your arms and shoulders in a neutral position. Pair this with an ergonomic chair that provides correct lumbar support, allowing your spine to remain in its natural posture.

Another key ergonomic aspect is monitor positioning. Your screen should be at eye level, about 20-30 inches away from your face, so you don't have to twist your head or strain your vision. Keep your keyboard and mouse at a comfortable height, and your wrists in a neutral position, to reduce strain. Wrist rests or an ergonomic mouse can help with comfort. Finally, take frequent breaks to stretch, walk around, and modify your posture during the day. This promotes physical health and mental clarity.

## The Importance of Proper Lighting

A well-lit home office can have a significant impact on productivity and well-being. Poor lighting can cause eye strain, headaches, and a general feeling of discomfort, while good lighting creates a more pleasant and energized workspace. Ideally, your office should receive ample natural light, as exposure to daylight is known to boost mood and energy levels. Place your desk near a window to take advantage of this, but make sure to avoid direct sunlight, which can cause glare on your screen.

In addition to natural light, task lighting is required for detailed tasks like reading or writing. A desk lamp with adjustable brightness allows you to customize the amount of light in your workspace. Choose gentle, warm lighting to create a peaceful atmosphere. Additionally, ensure that the entire space is equally lighted with overhead lights or wall-mounted bulbs, and avoid strong fluorescent lights, which can cause eye strain. If natural light is restricted, try utilizing full-spectrum light bulbs that replicate daylight to keep your workspace healthy and bright.

## Organization: Decluttering for Focus and Efficiency

A messy desk might impair your ability to concentrate and remain productive. In contrast, a well-organized home office encourages clarity of thought and efficiency. To accomplish this, use efficient storage solutions to keep paperwork, office supplies, and equipment properly organized. Shelves, filing cabinets, and storage bins can all help you achieve a minimalist, distraction-free atmosphere.

Cable management is another important aspect of office organization. Use cable clips or trays to keep wires neatly buried and out of the way. Desk accessories, such as pen and notepad organizers, can also assist keep your workstation organized. At the conclusion of each workday, take a few measures to tidy up your desk so you can begin the next day with a clean and uncluttered workstation.

## Aesthetics: Designing a Space You Love

Your home office should be more than just a functional space; it should also be enjoyable to spend time in. The aesthetics of your workspace can influence your mood and creativity, so it's critical to personalize it with deliberate design choices. Start by choosing a color scheme that enhances the atmosphere you wish to cultivate. Calming, neutral tones like blues, greens, or soft grays help relieve stress, while bolder accent colors can inject energy and vibrancy into the room.

Bringing plants inside your office can also help the environment. Plants not only enhance air quality, but they also provide a natural element to the space, making it more peaceful and inviting. Low-maintenance plants like succulents and snake plants are ideal for busy remote workers. When it comes to design, choose artwork, images, or motivational quotations that encourage you, but avoid overcrowding your room with too many stuff, which can cause visual clutter.

**Technology: Optimizing Your Workflow**

In addition to aesthetics and organization, having the appropriate technology in your home office is critical for optimizing your workflow. High-speed internet is required for remote work to ensure smooth video conversations, online collaboration, and quick access to cloud-based solutions. Make sure your home office is within range of your Wi-Fi router, or use a cable connection if necessary, for the best speed and reliability.

Your computer configuration is another critical factor. Depending on your work requirements, invest in a laptop or desktop with sufficient processing power to complete your activities successfully. If you do a lot of multitasking or need to pay attention to detail, consider adding another monitor. A multifunction printer and scanner can help those who deal with papers on a regular basis save time and effort. Wireless options are particularly useful for reducing clutter. Don't forget to preserve your technology investments by employing a surge protector to prevent power fluctuations.

**Sound Management: Reducing Noise Distractions**

Working from home frequently involves coping with a range of noisy disturbances, whether from family members, neighbors, or street activity. Effective sound management can help you stay focused and minimize distractions. Noise-canceling headphones are an excellent purchase for reducing background noise and allowing you to focus on your work. If you want a more long-term option, soundproofing your home office with heavy drapes, rugs, or acoustic panels can help limit outside noise.

A white noise machine or a simple phone app can also help to mask annoying noises and create a more serene working atmosphere. If your job necessitates quiet for critical calls or meetings, disclose your schedule to household members so they can reduce noise during these hours.

**Designing for Flexibility**

Finally, when designing your home office, keep flexibility in mind. Your requirements may alter over time, whether owing to job changes, the installation of new equipment, or simply a desire for a different workplace. Choose modular furniture that can be quickly rearranged or altered, like a height-adjustable desk or a foldable table. Mobile storage containers on wheels can also be moved as needed, allowing you to easily adjust your office arrangement.

For individuals with limited space, constructing a dual-purpose workplace is an excellent approach to maximise functionality. For example, a guest room can double as your desk while not in use, and a little area of the living room can change into an effective office space with the right furniture and organization.

Designing the ideal home office entails designing a setting that not only looks good but also promotes your work style, productivity, and well-being. By considering factors such as location, ergonomics, lighting, organization, aesthetics, technology, sound management, and flexibility, you can create a home office that suits your needs and helps you to operate at your peak.

# The Power of a Morning Routine

Creating an organized and productive morning ritual is one of the most potent ways to start the day on a positive note. This is especially crucial for remote workers, who frequently lack the natural structure that a regular office environment offers. Create a personalized routine that works for you to start the day with more clarity, energy, and focus. In this chapter, we'll look at the science behind morning routines, the primary benefits, and how to create one that boosts productivity and well-being.

**Why Morning Routines Matter**

A morning routine is more than just a series of activities; it provides consistency and predictability, which are critical for self-motivation and maintaining equilibrium. Routines that assist structure the day are especially beneficial to remote workers. When you stick to a morning routine, your brain transitions smoothly from one task to the next, boosting both mental clarity and efficiency.

A well-structured regimen can provide several major benefits. First, it increases productivity by beginning the day with purpose and focus, laying the groundwork for more efficient task management throughout the day. Second, it can benefit mental health by lowering worry and stress. A routine gives you a sense of control, which can help lessen the unpredictability and overwhelm that often come with remote work. Furthermore, a routine can boost your energy levels, especially if it incorporates activities like exercise or mindfulness, which assist to wake up the body and mind. Finally, a morning routine can improve work-life balance by allowing you to focus on self-care and personal priorities before getting into the grind of your professional day.

These benefits are supported by scientific evidence. According to research, morning rituals assist manage circadian rhythms, or our internal body clocks, which influence our mood, alertness, and overall health. Maintaining a consistent schedule reinforces positive behaviors, which contribute to long-term well-being.

## Key Components of an Effective Morning Routine

An efficient morning routine gets you psychologically and physically ready for the day ahead. Let's look at some key components to consider including into your practice.

1. Wake up early and consistently.

Getting up at the same time every day is one of the most critical aspects of a good habit. Consistency helps control your sleep cycle, allowing your body to naturally wake up and stay aware throughout the day. To make getting up simpler, establish a consistent bedtime that allows you enough rest. Avoid hitting the snooze button because it can disturb your sleep pattern and make you feel tired.

2. Hydrate your body.

Following several hours of sleep, your body becomes dehydrated, which might impair your ability to concentrate. Drinking water first thing in the morning is an easy but effective strategy to rehydrate and boost your metabolism. Keep a glass of water near your bed to consume as soon as you wake up. For an added kick, mix lemon or cucumber into your water for a vitamin-rich start.

3. Incorporate Physical Activity.

Morning exercise boosts blood flow, wakes up your muscles, and produces endorphins, all of which improve your mood and reduce stress. Moving your body, whether through yoga, a brisk stroll, or a fast cardio exercise, prepares you for the day ahead. Even gentle stretching or a few minutes of bodyweight exercises can greatly improve energy and focus.

4. Practice mindfulness or meditation.

Taking a few moments to practice mindfulness can have a long-term influence on your mental clarity and emotional equilibrium. Meditation, deep breathing, and writing are all mindfulness techniques that can help you focus and reduce stress. Begin with only five minutes of focusing on your breath or thinking about something you're grateful for. This establishes a positive, peaceful tone for the remainder of the day.

5. Plan and Prioritize Your Day.

Before you begin work, spend some time to arrange your ideas and plan your day. Make a to-do list of the most important chores to complete and prioritize them accordingly. You can also utilize time-blocking strategies to designate particular times to tasks, which discourages multitasking and keeps you on track. Setting intentions for the day, such as how you want to feel or what you want to accomplish, can give your actions greater purpose and significance.

6. Eat a nutritious breakfast.

Breakfast is an essential component of your morning routine, giving the energy and nutrition need to power your body and mind. A well-balanced dinner with protein, fiber, and healthy fats helps you maintain energy and concentrate until lunchtime. Smoothies, porridge with fruit, and eggs with avocado toast are all excellent options for a nutritious, full start to the day.

**Creating Your Ideal Morning Routine**

Creating a morning routine that works for you requires time and experimentation. Start small by introducing one or two new habits into your morning routine. For example, you could start your day with a glass of water and a short stretch. Once these routines become second nature, you can gradually incorporate new hobbies, such as meditation or a brief workout. Starting modest helps you avoid feeling overwhelmed and boosts your chances of success.

Flexibility is also important. While consistency is key, it's also critical to alter your regimen as needed. Some mornings may be busier than others, and life's unforeseen happenings can derail even the finest planned. In certain circumstances, prioritize basic actions such as hydration and planning, and modify the remainder of your schedule as needed.

Finally, monitor your development. Keeping a notebook or utilizing an app to document daily routine can help you think about what works and what doesn't. Over time, you'll uncover a set of routines that leave you feeling energized, focused, and ready to face the day.

## Benefits of a Morning Routine for Remote Workers

Establishing a morning routine is especially important for remote workers because it gives the structure they need to stay productive and balanced throughout the day. A well-planned routine improves focus by preparing your brain for work, allowing you to begin with clarity and a sense of purpose. It also helps time management, helping you to better arrange your responsibilities and minimize distractions associated with working from home. Furthermore, a morning routine reduces stress by instilling a sense of calm and control, especially when it combines mindfulness and planning components. Perhaps most crucially, it aids in the maintenance of work-life balance by putting self-care and personal well-being first before the demands of the job.

A morning ritual is an effective way to start your day with intention and enthusiasm. Whether your regimen lasts 30 minutes or two hours, the objective is to develop habits that prepare you emotionally and physically for the challenges ahead. A morning routine gives the discipline and stability that remote workers require to succeed, as their days can frequently feel unstructured. By adhering to the concepts presented in this chapter, you may develop a routine that suits your own lifestyle, allowing you to feel more productive, motivated, and in charge every day.

# Creating a Daily Schedule That Works

Designing a daily schedule that combines productivity and well-being is critical for remote employees. Without the framework of a physical office or set hours, work can easily flow over into personal time, resulting in fatigue or procrastination. A well-planned schedule offers the structure for staying focused, managing time efficiently, and setting clear boundaries between work and personal life. In this chapter, we'll look at how to create an effective daily plan that's personalized to your specific needs, with a focus on identifying priorities, increasing flexibility, and maintaining a healthy work-life balance.

**Why a Daily Schedule is Important**

A daily plan is more than simply a routine; it's a tool that remote workers can employ to boost productivity, reduce stress, and strike a work-life balance. Remote employment, which lacks the physical limits of an office and defined work hours, can easily blur the borders between home and work. A set timetable allows you to focus on your job without overworking or neglecting crucial personal responsibilities.

First and foremost, following a daily routine increases productivity. You may do more in less time by scheduling your most critical chores around when your energy and focus are at their optimum. A timetable also reduces stress since knowing what your day will look like and when you will complete particular activities gives you a sense of order and control. Finally, a daily schedule is vital for achieving work-life balance by ensuring that work does not occupy all of your time while also leaving time for hobbies, family, and pleasure.

**Key Elements of an Effective Daily Schedule**

An efficient daily calendar is more than just a to-do list; it is a well-balanced plan that considers your energy levels, the need for breaks, and unexpected jobs. We discuss the main components of a strong daily routine for remote work.

1. Morning Routine.

The way you start your day can frequently determine how successful it will be. A consistent morning ritual prepares your body and mind for the day ahead, instilling a sense of serenity and readiness. Whether you begin your day with a glass of water, a small workout, or a minute to evaluate your goals, this practice sets the tone for a productive day.

For example, you might include:

Hydrating and having a healthy breakfast.

Engaging in some form of movement, such as stretching or walking.

Reviewing your to-do list and setting goals for the day.

2) Prioritization

Not all tasks are created equal, and efficient prioritization is critical for optimal productivity. To properly prioritize tasks, consider the Eisenhower Matrix, which separates them into four quadrants depending on urgency and importance. Concentrate first on jobs that are both urgent and important. Another method is time blocking, in which you set aside particular times to work on high-priority projects, ensuring they have your complete attention.

3. Time Blocking.

Time blocking is an effective time management method that entails arranging certain blocks of time for various tasks. Instead of going through an endless to-do list, you set aside time for concentrated work, meetings, or personal tasks. For example, your morning might be like this:

Morning routine: 8:00 a.m. to 9:00 a.m.

9:00 AM - 11:00 AM: Concentrated efforts on a high-priority project.

11:00 a.m. to 12:00 p.m.: Respond to emails or attend meetings.

This method ensures that each task receives the attention it requires without distraction.

4. Built-In Breaks

Continuous work without pauses can cause weariness, burnout, and decreased concentration. Taking regular breaks is essential for maintaining mental clarity and efficiency. One example is the Pomodoro Technique, which involves working for 25 minutes and then taking a 5-minute rest. Longer breaks, such as a 30-minute lunch or a 15-20-minute stroll, can help you re-energize for the rest of the day.

5. Flexibility for unexpected tasks

While structure is necessary, flexibility is also essential when managing a remote work schedule. Life happens, and unexpected responsibilities or obstacles can come throughout the day. Building buffer time into your plan allows you to deal with distractions without disrupting your entire day. Adding a 15-30 minute buffer between big tasks or setting aside catch-up time at the end of the day guarantees that you can handle any unexpected events.

6. End-of-Day Routine.

Just as starting your day with intention is vital, ending it with a routine aids in the shift from work mentality to personal time. An end-of-day routine can include reviewing what you completed, identifying any activities that need to be carried over to the next day, and establishing priorities for tomorrow. Disconnecting from work emails and notifications during this time allows you to completely unwind and recuperate.

**Creating Your Personalized Daily Schedule**

Creating a daily plan that actually works for you necessitates a personalized strategy in which you experiment with various ways and make adjustments based on your energy levels, work obligations, and personal life. Here's how to make a personalized schedule:

1. Determine your most productive times. Everyone has various peak production times. Some people are more concentrated in the morning, while others discover their rhythm later in the day. Monitor your energy and focus levels throughout the day, and schedule your most difficult tasks for those peak hours.

2. Include Non-Negotiable Tasks. Identify everyday duties, such as meetings, deadlines, or personal responsibilities, and schedule them first. This guarantees that you account for them and avoids last-minute scheduling issues.

3. Schedule time for deep work. Deep work is focused, continuous work that necessitates considerable mental effort. To maximize production, set aside time for intensive work during your most productive hours and avoid distractions.

4. Increase breaks and buffer time. Include short and long breaks to refuel, and provide for buffer time between jobs to account for overruns or unforeseen disruptions.

5. Review and adjust. No timetable is ideal from the beginning. After following your program for a week or two, assess its effectiveness. Are you being productive or feeling overwhelmed? Adjust the timetable to better suit your natural work cycle and personal life.

A carefully planned daily schedule has significant advantages for remote workers. It improves focus by allowing you to concentrate on one topic at a time without distractions. It prevents procrastination by providing a precise schedule for the day, allowing less room for delays. It also enhances work-life balance by preventing work from spilling over into personal time and setting clear boundaries. Finally, executing activities as intended gives you a sense of success and satisfaction, which promotes motivation and confidence.

Creating a unique daily plan is an ongoing process of discovering what works best for you, both professionally and personally. Prioritization, time blocking, and flexibility may all be used to design a timetable that allows you to stay productive while still keeping a healthy balance. With consistency and regular review, your daily plan can become a helpful tool for thriving in a remote work setting.

# Effective Time Blocking for Remote Workers

Time blocking is an effective time management method, especially for remote workers who confront unique obstacles in remaining productive while maintaining a healthy work-life balance. This strategy is partitioning your day into discrete blocks of time, each committed to a single work or activity. By setting up specific times for work, breaks, and personal activities, you can avoid distractions, focus more deeply, and manage your day more efficiently.

Unlike standard to-do lists, which frequently result in multitasking or bouncing between tasks, time blocking promotes focused work. Time blocking assigns a specific time to each activity, which aids in avoiding common productivity traps such as procrastination, distractions, and the overwhelming sense of having too much to do. Let's look deeper into how time blocking works, its multiple benefits, and how to properly include it into your remote work routine.

**What is Time Blocking?**

At its core, time blocking is a scheduling approach in which you divide your day into time blocks, each of which is reserved for a certain activity or collection of tasks. Instead of working from an unstructured list, you designate a specific time for focused work, meetings, administrative tasks, and even personal activities like exercise or leisure. For example, you may set aside time in the morning for intense work, such as focusing on a major project, followed by time for answering emails or holding client meetings.

A typical day using time blocking might look something like this:

8:00 AM - 8:30 AM: Morning routine

8:30 AM - 10:30 AM: Deep work on a critical project

10:30 AM - 11:00 AM: Respond to emails

11:00 AM - 12:00 PM: Client meeting

12:00 PM - 1:00 PM: Lunch break

1:00 PM - 2:30 PM: Continue working on the project

2:30 PM - 3:00 PM: Social media outreach

3:00 PM - 4:00 PM: Administrative tasks and task review

4:00 PM - 5:00 PM: Personal time or errands

By allocating certain time periods to specific tasks, you not only establish an organized day, but also let yourself to focus on one activity at a time, increasing productivity and decreasing the mental load of continually determining what to do next.

**Why Time Blocking is Beneficial for Remote Workers**

Remote workers often have more flexibility in their schedules than those in regular office settings. However, with such independence comes the risk of developing bad work habits like distractions, procrastination, and overworking. Time blocking provides much-needed structure and discipline, increasing remote workers' efficiency while also encouraging a healthier work-life balance.

One of the key advantages of time blocking is higher productivity. Multitasking—attempting to manage multiple activities at once—divides your attention, resulting in mistakes, longer completion times, and overall inefficiency. Time blocking enables you to devote your complete focus to one task at a time, thereby boosting the quality and speed of your output.

Another significant benefit is that time blocking helps to define clearer work-life boundaries. For remote professionals, particularly those who work from home, the distinction between work and personal life might be blurred. Without proper planning, you may find yourself working late at night or running personal errands during business hours. Time blocking guarantees that you schedule certain hours for work and personal activities, allowing you to maintain a healthy balance.

Furthermore, time blocking helps to boost focus. You can reduce distractions and interruptions by setting out certain blocks of time for focused work, such as creative pursuits, writing, or programming. Instead than continuously checking emails or being pulled into unplanned meetings, you can schedule these chores outside of your most productive hours. This level of focus not only boosts output but also makes work more satisfying.

Additionally, time blocking promotes better time management. When you plan your day in advance, you reduce the inefficiency of determining what to work on next, resulting in more deliberate use of your time. Finally, it minimizes decision fatigue, which is the mental strain caused by making constant decisions during the day. With time blocks in place, you know exactly what you'll be working on and when, making moving from one activity to the next much easier.

## How to Implement Time Blocking Effectively

To properly include time blocking into your routine, you'll need a clear strategy. Here's a step-by-step tutorial to get you started:

The first step is to determine your priorities. Before you can schedule time, you must first identify your major objectives and goals. Make a list of your most important chores, such as big projects, client work, and deadlines, as well as your regular tasks, such as emails, meetings, and administrative duties. Don't forget to add personal activities like exercise and family time. Recognizing your priorities allows you to devote the most productive time of your day to the most critical things.

Next, divide complex jobs into digestible bits. It is easy to become overwhelmed by large projects, which frequently leads to procrastination. To avoid this, divide major jobs into smaller, more achievable steps that can be completed within a specific time frame. For example, instead of setting out a whole morning to "work on project," divide it into different blocks for research, drafting, and editing.

Once you've separated your responsibilities, set aside time for intensive work during your peak production hours. Deep work refers to jobs that need deep focus with little distractions. For many people, the morning is the most productive time of day, so it's a good idea to set out this time for focused work. Set aside at least 1-2 hours to focus without interruptions.

Also, remember to give a buffer period between blocks. Avoid scheduling consecutive chores without breaks. Having 5-15 minute buffer periods helps you to reset, get a food, or deal with any unexpected complications. These brief pauses minimize burnout and keep you on track throughout the day.

Finally, remember to set boundaries for breaks and personal time. Time blocking is more than just working effectively; it's also about striking a balance between work and rest. Take regular pauses and engage in personal activities to refuel during the day. Whether it's a stroll, lunch, or time with family, these personal time blocks are critical for long-term productivity and well-being.

**Types of Time Blocks**

Not all tasks demand the same amount of concentration or time investment, which is why different sorts of time blocks might be useful. Here are some sorts you can include in your schedule:

Focus Blocks are reserved for intense activity that requires your whole attention. These blocks are typically 60-90 minutes long, as research indicates that this is the best time for sustained concentration. Use these times for high-priority jobs like writing, coding, or other creative activity.

Admin Blocks are used for normal operations such as checking emails, scheduling meetings, and organizing papers. Because these jobs do not demand strong concentration, they can be planned for lower-energy times of day, such as the afternoon.

Meeting Blocks are allotted for video calls or phone meetings, which are frequently required in remote work environments. Scheduling all of your meetings in one block helps to keep them from interrupting your intense work. Try to keep them in defined time periods to avoid spreading them out throughout the day.

Finally, personal time blocks are as vital. These include self-care, exercise, and family time. Personal time limits ensure that work does not consume your entire day, allowing you to live a balanced and healthy lifestyle.

**Common Pitfalls and How to Avoid Them**

While time blocking is quite successful, there are a few frequent drawbacks that might negate its advantages. One of the most common faults is over scheduling, which involves filling every minute of the day with work. This provides no room for unforeseen problems or much-needed downtime. Always leave some room in your calendar for unexpected events or to simply unwind.

Another common concern is giving exaggerated time estimates. It's easy to underestimate how long things will take, which can lead to anger when they're not completed on time. To avoid this, provide ample time estimates, particularly for difficult activities.

Finally, resist the need to deviate from your routine too frequently. While it is necessary to be adaptable, frequently deviating from your plans might result in a loss of structure and productivity. Stick to your schedule as much as possible, making adjustments only when absolutely necessary.

**Tracking and Refining Your Time Blocking**

Time blocking, like any other productivity method, requires improvement. Monitor your progress over a few weeks to see what works and what doesn't. Consider whether your time predictions were correct, if particular blocks overlapped, or if you felt rushed. Use this information to improve your calendar and make time blocking more successful for your specific work style.

Time blocking is a versatile and useful strategy, particularly for remote workers looking to better manage their time. By establishing scheduled, intentional blocks for concentrated work, meetings, and personal duties, you may increase productivity, reduce stress, and achieve a healthy work/life balance. The key to success is consistency—sticking to your schedule while remaining adaptable to life's unavoidable changes. With practice, time blocking can change the way you work, allowing you to do more in less time while living a satisfying and balanced life.

# Managing Distractions and Staying Focused

Managing distractions is a key difficulty for remote workers, as the convenience of working from home frequently comes with a slew of interruptions and temptations that can stymie productivity. Without the constraints of a regular office setting, it's easy to lose focus due to household duties, social media, or unexpected interruptions. However, with the correct tactics, you may efficiently minimize distractions and establish a more focused and productive work habit. In this chapter, we'll look at why distractions happen, what the most prevalent distractions are for remote workers, and how to resist them.

## Understanding Why Distractions Happen

Distractions are unavoidable, but they appear to be more common in remote work contexts. Without the external structure of an office, such as colleagues and a set workstation, it is easy to become distracted. One of the most common causes of distractions is a lack of organization. In an office, there are clear signals that it is time to work—commuting, scheduled meetings, and coworkers all contribute to a work-focused environment. However, working from home blurs these distinctions, making it harder to maintain the same degree of concentration.

Another important component is consistent connectivity. The growth of technology, including social media, email, and messaging apps, has resulted in a flood of notifications that can disrupt deep work. Each ping or alarm diverts your attention away from your present task, making it difficult to focus. Similarly, procrastination is a distraction that frequently stems from within. When faced with a difficult or tiresome activity, it's tempting to procrastinate by turning to easier, more fun distractions, such as browsing the internet or checking your phone. Finally, multitasking is a common problem. While hopping between jobs may appear to be productive, it divides your concentration and diminishes your overall productivity.

**Common Distractions for Remote Workers**

For remote workers, distractions can take many forms, some of which are specific to the home environment. Household chores and errands are a common issue. The flexibility of remote work can make it tempting to tackle small household tasks throughout the day, but these activities can quickly eat into your work time. Family or roommate interruptions are another challenge. If you live with others, it can be difficult to avoid being interrupted by casual conversations or questions, especially if they don't fully understand your work schedule.

Social media and the internet are also significant sources of distraction. With a few clicks, you can easily spend hours scrolling through Instagram, reading the news, or watching videos. Small distractions can easily accumulate, drastically limiting productivity. Even emails and notifications, which are work-related, might be a distraction. Checking and responding to emails or texts all day disrupts your focus and can impede your progress on larger assignments. Finally, noisy neighbors, street traffic, or a cluttered setting can all make it difficult to concentrate. Without a specific workspace, it can be difficult to truly enter "work mode."

**Proven Strategies to Manage Distractions**

Fortunately, there are numerous successful ways that remote workers can employ to control distractions and maintain focus. One of the most successful solutions is to set up a dedicated workstation. Whether it's a home office, a specialized workstation, or a section of your living room, having a designated work location can help you separate your business and personal lives. A clean, orderly workspace free of distractions tells your brain that it's time to work, making it simpler to concentrate.

Another effective time management tool is the Pomodoro Technique, which entails working in small, focused bursts of 25 minutes each, followed by a 5-minute rest. This method helps you keep concentration by dividing down your job into small portions and avoiding burnout. Working for a specific period of time and then taking a short break allows you to avoid distractions and maintain your energy levels throughout the day.

To further decrease distractions, turn off notifications. Disabling notifications from non-essential apps during work hours will help you avoid repeated disruptions. Set your phone on "Do Not Disturb" mode and set particular times to read your email or texts, rather than responding to every notice as it arrives.

If social networking or browsing the internet is a major distraction for you, consider employing website blockers such as StayFocusd or Freedom. These solutions allow you to prevent access to distracting websites during work hours or limit the amount of time you can spend on non-work-related websites. This helps you stay focused and avoid getting diverted.

Establishing a routine is another important method for dealing with distractions. Creating a consistent daily schedule provides structure and helps you stay on target. Begin your day with a morning ritual, set regular work hours, and schedule breaks to refresh. This constancy makes it easy to get in and out of work mode, even when working from home.

Clear communication with family and housemates is also vital. Tell individuals around you about your work routine and when you require undisturbed time. This can be accomplished through verbal agreements or physical cues, such as closing the door or displaying a sign during a meeting or focused work session. Setting these boundaries reduces disruptions and ensures that your working hours are respected.

Finally, mindfulness can help you handle internal distractions. Mindfulness is the practice of remaining present and completely focused in the job at hand. By honing this skill, you can become more aware of when your mind wanders and gently return your focus back to your tasks. Mindfulness techniques like deep breathing or short meditation sessions before work can help you focus and manage distractions better.

**Maintaining Focus Over the Long Term**

While controlling distractions on a daily basis is vital, maintaining attention over time demands consistent effort. One important method is to routinely assess your productivity. At the end of each week, assess how well you handled interruptions and determine which tactics worked best. This reflection enables you to consistently enhance your attention and productivity.

Taking regular breaks is also important for staying focused. Working continuously can lead to burnout, making it difficult to concentrate over time. Taking breaks from your desk, whether for a walk, stretching, or a snack, refreshes your mind and allows you to return to work with newfound enthusiasm.

Finally, maintain your flexibility. Even with the finest planning, distractions will inevitably occur. The goal is to remain adaptable and not become discouraged by unexpected interruptions. When a distraction happens, refocus as soon as possible and return to your work.

Managing distractions is one of the most difficult issues for remote workers, but with the correct tactics, it is possible to stay focused and productive. You may reclaim control of your attention and avoid interruptions by setting up a dedicated workplace, employing techniques such as the Pomodoro method, shutting off notifications, setting clear boundaries with others around you, and practicing mindfulness.

Focus is a skill that may be improved through practice. By constantly implementing these tactics, you will improve your ability to concentrate, decrease distractions, and make the most of your remote workday, ultimately increasing your productivity and overall work-life balance.

# Dealing with Family and Household Interruptions

Working from home provides great flexibility and freedom, but it also presents problems, notably in managing family and household disruptions. Whether you live with a partner, children, or roommates, these distractions can disrupt your concentration and make it difficult to finish activities efficiently. This chapter will look at why domestic interruptions happen, how they affect your work, and practical ways for reducing and managing them—all while preserving great relationships with your family or housemates.

## The Nature of Household Interruptions

Household interruptions differ from job disruptions in that they originate in your personal environment. Interruptions in a traditional office are often caused by coworkers, meetings, or unexpected phone calls, whereas they might be more varied and frequent at home. Family members, domestic activities, and environmental diversions all contribute to this problem.

One of the most typical complaints is about family interruptions. Your husband or children may impulsively ask for assistance or attempt to engage you in conversation, drawing you away from your task. If you're the go-to person for problem solving in your household, you'll probably encounter these distractions more frequently.

Chores and errands are another common cause of disruptions. Being at home makes it appealing to perform housework, whether it's laundry, tidying up, or running errands. These chores, while vital, might disrupt your workflow when completed during business hours.

Environmental distractions, such as noise from family members, pets, or external sounds like traffic, can also interfere with attention. For parents with small children, juggling childcare with work commitments can be especially difficult, especially if clear limits have not been set.

## The Impact of Household Interruptions on Remote Work

Even minor household interruptions can have a substantial impact on productivity and attention. One of the major concerns is a phenomena known as "attention residue," in which your mind remains focused on the interruption even after you have returned to your activity. It takes effort to regain attention, and many distractions exacerbate the problem.

### The impacts are wide-reaching:

Reduced Productivity: Frequent interruptions result in fragmented work, which causes delays in job completion and makes it difficult to maintain a consistent workflow. With each interruption, your focus shifts, making you less productive.

Increased Stress: Juggling work commitments and family obligations can be tough. Constant interruptions can cause annoyance, anxiety, and even guilt because you feel like you're neglecting work or family.

Loss of Focus: Each interruption disrupts your focus, and it takes time to regain a productive mental state. This can be especially difficult if you're engaged on intricate chores that need intense concentration.

Extended Work Hours: To make up for missed time owing to distractions, many remote workers wind up working more hours. This can disrupt work-life balance, leaving little time for relaxation or meaningful time with family.

## Strategies for Managing Family and Household Interruptions

To deal with home interruptions, set boundaries, communicate effectively, and create an organized environment. The following are practical ways for reducing distractions and maintaining a work-life balance.

1. Create clear work boundaries.

The first step toward reducing interruptions is to draw clear lines between your job and personal lives. Your family or housemates must realize that you are "at work" and should not be interrupted until absolutely required.

Designate Work Hours: Make a set timetable for your working hours and convey it clearly to your family. During these times, make it clear that you are unavailable for non-emergency disruptions.

Use Visual cues: Simple visual cues, like as closing the door to your office or wearing headphones, might suggest that you are concentrated and should not be bothered. These signs can serve as reminders that you are in business mode.

Communicate Expectations: Have open conversations with your family about what qualifies as an emergency and when it's appropriate to interrupt you. For example, smaller requests can wait until a break, while urgent matters may require immediate attention.

2. Create a Daily Routine for Your Family

Just as having a structured routine is important for your own productivity, it can also help manage your family's activities. Aligning their routine with your work schedule can minimize disruptions during critical work hours.

Set Activity Times for Kids: If you have children, arrange independent playtime or educational activities during your busiest work hours. Engaging them in mentally stimulating or enjoyable tasks will keep them occupied while you work.

Meal and Break Schedules: Plan meal and snack times to coincide with your work breaks. This will provide you allocated time to spend with your family, ensuring that they do not disturb you for minor requirements during working hours.

Assign domestic duties: Divide domestic duties among family members or schedule them outside of work hours. By doing chores outside of work hours, you limit the desire to do them while working.

3. Use time blocking for family and work tasks.

Time blocking is a strong productivity approach in which you set up particular time intervals for various activities. You may apply this to both your professional and family commitments to create a well-structured day with no overlap.

Block Family Time: Schedule specified hours for family activities or conversations. When your family knows there is a set time for them, they are less likely to disrupt you during work hours.

Schedule short breaks to complete little housekeeping tasks. Rather than allowing these responsibilities to disrupt your workflow, use these intervals to do required tasks such as cleaning up or preparing a meal.

4. Create a dedicated workspace.

Having a distinct workstation is critical for staying focused and avoiding distractions. A dedicated workspace can help you mentally divide your professional and personal lives, allowing you to stay focused during work hours.

Location: Select a workspace away from high-traffic sections of the home, such as the kitchen or living room. A calmer, more secluded location will minimize noise and distractions.

Ergonomics: Ensure that your workspace is comfortable and productive. Invest in a comfortable chair, desk, and lighting so you can work comfortably for long periods of time.

Boundaries: Set up your office in a room with a door that can be closed. This provides a physical barrier, indicating to your family that you are working and should not be disturbed.

5. Establish communication protocols.

To manage interruptions, maintain regular communication with your family or housemates. Having open discussions about timetables, expectations, and obligations will allow everyone to coexist harmoniously in the same area.

Family gatherings: Schedule frequent family gatherings to address your job schedule and domestic requirements. This is an excellent time to ensure that everyone is on the same page and resolve any issues.

Set Emergency Protocols: Create a clear strategy for crises so that your family understands when and how to contact you if necessary. This decreases the possibility of minor concerns being classified as urgent.

Use a Visual Schedule: Posting a shared schedule in a common place, such as on the refrigerator, may keep everyone up to date on your work hours and availability.

6. Leverage Childcare Solutions

For parents with young children, balancing work and daycare is frequently the most difficult component of remote work. There are numerous options for allowing you to focus on your career while still safeguarding your children's well-being.

Partner Shifts: If you have a partner, schedule shifts in which one person works while the other cares for the children. This rotating timetable provides each of you with uninterrupted work time.

Hire Help: If possible, hire a babysitter or ask a family member to help with childcare during your hardest working hours. This can provide you with the necessary time and space to focus without distractions.

Create a Child-Friendly workstation: If hiring help is not an option, set up a small play area near your workstation for your children to play independently. This allows you to keep an eye on them while also getting things done.

**Maintaining a Healthy Work-Life Balance.**

While dealing with domestic interruptions is vital, so is maintaining a healthy work-life balance. Remote work allows for greater freedom, but without clear boundaries and routines, the distinctions between work and home life can get blurred.

Be Flexible When Necessary: Regardless of your best efforts, interruptions will occur. Try to maintain your flexibility and adaptability. A quick request from your child or an unanticipated home issue may require immediate attention, which is acceptable.

Set realistic expectations: Recognize that working from home presents unique challenges, and it may not always be able to perform every task as effectively as in an office setting. Establish realistic goals and be gentle with yourself.

Practice Self-Care: Balancing work and family can be difficult, so make time for yourself. Self-care, whether through exercise, meditation, or simply relaxing, helps to combat burnout and keeps you refreshed for work and family life.

Household disruptions are a typical issue for remote workers, but with the correct tactics, they may be effectively addressed. Clear communication, disciplined routines, and well-defined boundaries are essential for fostering a more productive and harmonious remote work environment. You can prosper both at work and at home by incorporating your family in the process and making strategic adjustments to your work habits. With these strategies, you can benefit from the freedom of remote work while keeping healthy relationships with your loved ones and remaining productive.

# Lunch Break and Downtime: Why You Need Them

When working remotely, it's tempting to fall into the habit of missing breaks, particularly lunch breaks, in the hope that working through them will boost productivity. However, the contrary is true. Taking regular breaks, especially adequate lunch breaks and intentional rest, is critical for sustaining long-term productivity, creativity, and general health. This chapter looks at why breaks are important, the research behind their advantages, and how to properly include them into your remote work schedule.

## The Importance of Breaks for Sustaining Productivity

One of the most common myths about productivity is that working longer hours without breaks leads to more work being completed. According to research, our brains were not built to focus on things for long periods of time without relaxation. Taking pauses boosts cognitive performance, improves focus, and lowers stress.

Working without breaks increases your risk of mental fatigue, which is caused by continuous focus without allowing your brain to rest. Mental tiredness can eventually lead to burnout, a chronic stress condition that impairs motivation, creativity, and vitality. Burnout is especially prevalent in remote work environments, where the lines between professional and personal life are frequently blurred.

Common symptoms of mental weariness and burnout include trouble concentrating, mental exhaustion, decreased motivation, and increased irritation. Regular breaks, particularly lunch breaks, help your brain to recover, minimizing burnout and maintaining your capacity to focus throughout the workday.

## The Advantages of Taking A Proper Lunch Break

Lunch breaks serve a much broader purpose than just feeding your body. They are critical for mental rest and preparation for the second half of the workday. Research indicates that taking a lunch break improves mental clarity, decision-making, and mood while also giving much-needed physical relaxation.

1. Physical Recovery.

Sitting at a computer for hours without moving can cause physical discomfort, such as neck, back, and eye strain. Taking a lunch break allows you to stretch, move around, and give your body the physical rest it need.

During your lunch break, incorporate brief stretching activities to relieve tension. A simple walk outside not only refreshes your body but also increases circulation and exposes you to sunlight, which can raise your mood and energy levels. To alleviate eye strain, take a break from screens and focus on distant objects.

2. Mental rejuvenation.

To perform properly, your brain, like your body, requires rest. Working continuously without taking breaks has a negative influence on cognitive capacities such as memory, problem solving, and decision making. A lunch break allows your brain to switch off from work mode, allowing you to return to your tasks with a new perspective and renewed energy.

Giving your mind time to relax can boost creativity, attention, and reduce stress. Many solutions to job problems emerge when you take a break and let your mind wander. After a lunch break, your concentration improves, making it simpler to do chores efficiently and successfully.

3. Social Connection.

Lunch breaks provide an opportunity to communicate with people, whether they be family members, roommates, or friends. Even brief social interactions can improve your mood and give you a sense of connectedness, which is especially important in a remote work setting. If you live alone, consider connecting digitally with friends or colleagues over lunchtime to alleviate feelings of isolation.

**The Science Behind Downtime: Why It's Necessary**

Incorporating downtime into your daily routine is essential for long-term health and productivity. Downtime is defined as any time when you take a break from work to rest your mind and body. It might be a lunch break, an afternoon rest, or some free time after work.

Cognitive Benefits of Downtime

Even when you're not actively working on a task, your brain continues to solve issues and develop ideas via what is known as the "default mode network." Downtime permits this network to function properly, allowing you to assimilate information, generate new ideas, and improve problem-solving skills.

Key cognitive benefits of downtime include enhanced problem-solving, memory consolidation, and increased innovation. Many creative ideas occur during moments of rest when your mind is free to wander and make connections. By taking regular breaks, you give your brain the time it needs to consolidate information and improve learning and recall.

Mental Health and Downtime

The absence of downtime can lead to feelings of overwhelm and contribute to burnout. Downtime provides the mental space necessary for reducing stress and improving overall mental health. Regular breaks from work help lower cortisol levels, reducing feelings of anxiety, and promoting a positive mood.

Incorporating leisure into your workday helps boost emotional resilience, allowing you to deal with workplace obstacles more effectively. Stepping away from work to rest and relax allows your mind to regenerate, which is essential for leading a balanced and healthy remote work life.

**How to Effectively Incorporate Breaks and Downtime.**

To get the most out of breaks and downtime, you must plan how you will spend them. Here are some ways for including successful breaks in your workday:

1. Schedule your lunch break.

Make your lunch break an essential part of your day. Set out a set time for it and step away from your workstation. Even if it's only for 30 minutes, this scheduled break will keep you from skipping or working through lunch. To reap the most restorative benefits, completely withdraw from work during this time.

2. Physically step away from your desk.

For a break to be successful, you must physically leave your workplace. Whether it's another room in your house or a quick walk outside, getting away from your work surroundings is essential for totally resetting your mind.

3. Practice mindfulness.

Practicing mindfulness during your lunch break or downtime can enhance its restorative benefits. Whether it's focusing on your meal without interruptions or taking a few deep breaths to calm yourself, mindfulness allows you to stay present and completely engaged during your break. This technique can boost the advantages of both short and long breaks, leaving you feeling rejuvenated and ready to return to work.

4. Plan Downtime Throughout Your Day

In addition to your lunch break, set aside specified times for shorter breaks or periods of rest, such as an afternoon break or after-work relaxation. Even a small 10-15 minute rest will greatly improve your energy and focus. Use this time to unwind, pursue hobbies, or simply rest to maintain your mental and emotional health.

**Practical Tips to Maximize Lunch Breaks and Downtime**

To make the most of your breaks, consider the following suggestions:

- Eat a Balanced Meal: Feed your body with nutritious foods to keep your energy levels steady and prevent mid-afternoon slumps.

- Move Around: Engage in light physical activity, such as walking or stretching, to refresh your body and relieve tension.

- Avoid Working During Breaks: Resist the urge to check emails or respond to messages while on break. Focus on rest and relaxation to make your vacation genuinely rejuvenating.

- Deep breathing, meditation, or simply listening to soothing music can all help you rest and recharge during your downtime.

- Take Micro-Breaks: In addition to lengthier breaks, take small (5-10 minute) micro-breaks throughout the day to stretch, refocus, and stay focused.

Including appropriate lunch breaks and frequent rest in your remote workplace is critical for maintaining productivity, creativity, and mental wellness. By taking a break from your desk and allowing your mind and body to relax, you will return to work with renewed focus, energy, and the ability to deal with obstacles more efficiently. In the long run, taking breaks not only boosts productivity but also promotes a good work-life balance, reducing burnout and fostering long-term success in your remote work journey.

# Mastering Communication with Remote Teams

Effective communication is the foundation for successful remote work. When team members are geographically distributed, it is even more important to ensure that everyone is on the same page, feels connected, and has access to the necessary information. Unlike in traditional offices, where informal face-to-face talks occur organically, distant communication necessitates greater intentionality, planning, and consistency. To accomplish this, remote teams must understand the particular obstacles they encounter and implement methods that promote clarity, engagement, and collaboration. This chapter digs into the challenges of remote team communication, best practices for keeping strong connections, and methods for facilitating collaboration in a distant environment.

## The Unique Challenges of Remote Communication

Remote communication provides unique issues when compared to in-person communication, owing to the lack of physical presence and overreliance on digital means. These difficulties, if not addressed effectively, can stymie collaboration, cause misunderstandings, and lower team morale.

One of the most major issues is the absence of nonverbal clues. Body language, facial gestures, and tone of voice all play an important role in conveying a message in person. Without these indicators in digital contexts, written communication can be easily misconstrued, resulting in misunderstanding and misalignment. This is especially true in messaging systems, where brief and speedy discussions may lack context or emotional complexity.

Time zone differences present another challenge. Remote teams are often spread across different regions, making it difficult to coordinate real-time communication. As a result, some team members may be working while others are offline, leading to delays in feedback or decision-making. This can make scheduling meetings and collaborating in real time more difficult.

Additionally, remote teams often experience an over-reliance on written communication. Email chains, messaging threads, and shared documents can become overwhelming, leading to information overload and misinterpretation. Moreover, important details can get lost in long message threads, creating confusion or inefficiencies as team members struggle to find relevant information.

Finally, information silos can arise in remote teams if communication is not well-organized or transparent. When team members or departments work independently without routinely sharing updates or resources, valuable information might become compartmentalized, resulting in duplication of effort or critical gaps in understanding. This issue is strongly related to feelings of isolation that remote workers may experience when communication is infrequent or impersonal, which can have an influence on team morale and participation.

## Best Practices For Effective Remote Communication

To overcome these issues, remote teams must use a set of best practices that encourage clarity, inclusivity, and effective cooperation. The following are some fundamental criteria for maintaining efficient communication in a remote team environment.

1. Set Clear Expectations

Setting clear expectations around communication is essential in remote teams. From the beginning, teams should agree on which channels to use for specific types of communication, establish response time expectations, and define guidelines for message formatting. For example, instant messaging might be best for quick updates, video calls for meetings, and emails for more detailed information. Clear communication norms help avoid misunderstandings and ensure consistency in how team members interact.

Additionally, setting reasonable response times for different communication channels is key to ensuring that team members know when to expect feedback. This could mean a 24-hour response time for emails and quicker replies for messages on platforms like Slack or Microsoft Teams.

2. Emphasize over-communication.

In a distant context, it's generally better to overcommunicate than to leave anything unexplained. Providing more context or background information, particularly in written communication, ensures that all team members have a complete picture. Team members should also be encouraged to check their comprehension of key messages by repeating them or asking clarifying questions. Following up on crucial talks with written summaries that include key insights and action items is an effective strategy to assure alignment and reduce the likelihood of misinterpretation.

3. Promote Transparency

Transparency is crucial in remote teams, because information can easily get segregated or lost. Leaders and team members should communicate regularly about their progress, issues, and any hurdles they face. This can be accomplished by doing daily or weekly check-ins, creating project dashboards, or providing status reports. Providing broad access to information via shared papers or project management software also guarantees that everyone is kept informed.

Furthermore, transparency includes creating an environment in which team members feel comfortable disclosing issues and asking for assistance. Creating a culture that encourages vulnerability fosters trust and guarantees that team members can lean on one another for help.

4. Use Video Conferencing For Important Conversations.

Written communication is handy, but it lacks the immediacy and emotional subtlety of in-person connection. For more sophisticated or sensitive interactions, video conferencing technologies such as Zoom, Google Meet, or Microsoft Teams allow you to evaluate tone, read facial expressions, and engage in real-time debate. Regular video meetings foster personal relationships, making team members feel more engaged and connected.

Schedule regular video check-ins, whether for status updates or informal discussions, to battle feelings of isolation. Encourage team members to move from written communication to video conversations when discussions grow too complex to guarantee that issues are addressed properly and quickly.

5. Be mindful of time zones.

It is critical to account everyone's schedule when working in remote teams across multiple time zones. This may include changing meeting schedules so that no single team member is routinely inconvenienced by early or late calls. Teams can use scheduling software such as World Time Buddy or Google Calendar to discover mutually accepted meeting hours.

Furthermore, asynchronous communication, in which team members participate to discussions or projects at different times, might be a useful solution for teams operating in separate time zones. Encourage asynchronous processes so that everyone can contribute and stay involved without having to be online at the same time.

6. Promote active listening.

Active listening is extremely crucial in remote teams to avoid misunderstandings and make sure everyone feels heard. Team members should be encouraged to fully listen to others before replying, as well as to ask clarifying questions. Restating essential points or summarizing a colleague's message is an effective way to check understanding.

Avoid interrupting people during video or phone calls. Encourage team members to wait until someone has done speaking before providing feedback to help keep the conversation respectful and helpful.

**Tools to Streamline Remote Communication**

Remote teams rely heavily on technology to facilitate communication. The correct tools may make cooperation easier and ensure that critical information is shared and available to everyone. Here are some of the best communication tools for remote teams:

1. Messaging platforms.

Tools like Slack and Microsoft Teams are extremely useful for real-time communication. They enable fast exchanges, direct texting, and organized conversations via channels. These platforms also provide file sharing and app integrations, which help to centralize communication.

2. Videoconferencing Tools

Zoom, Google Meet, and Microsoft Teams are popular video conferencing solutions that allow remote teams to hold face-to-face meetings wherever they are. Screen sharing, breakout rooms, and meeting records making them suitable for everything from daily check-ins to huge presentations.

3. Project Management Tools.

Project management software such as Trello, Asana, and Monday.com serve as a central center for teams to coordinate projects, measure progress, and keep organized. These platforms help to guarantee that everyone is on the same page about deadlines, responsibilities, and project updates, eliminating the possibility of misinterpretation.

4. Document Collaboration.

Google Drive, Dropbox Paper, and Microsoft OneDrive enable team members to collaborate on documents in real time. This ensures that everyone gets access to the most recent version of a document, avoiding the confusion of numerous file versions sent over email.

## Building a Strong Remote Team Culture Through Communication

Effective communication in remote teams involves more than just transferring information; it also entails developing a strong team culture. In a distant workplace where team members may feel alienated, facilitating social interaction and cultivating a sense of belonging can help to develop team bonds.

Virtual coffee breaks, in which team members can meet informally for non-work-related chats, are one method for developing rapport. Celebrating milestones like as birthdays and project completions promotes a sense of team spirit. Similarly, planning virtual team-building activities, such as online games or quizzes, can foster a fun, collaborative environment inside the team.

Any remote team's success depends on its ability to communicate effectively. Remote teams may develop excellent communication, increase productivity, and create a cohesive team culture by tackling common challenges, implementing best practices, and leveraging the correct tools. When communication is clear, regular, and inclusive, remote workers may cooperate effectively—often as efficiently as in a traditional office setting.

# The Role of Technology in Achieving Balance

In today's fast-paced digital world, technology is critical for remote workers seeking a healthy work-life balance. While modern tools' constant connectivity might blur the distinctions between professional and personal life, they also give countless resources that assist individuals in managing their time, prioritizing activities, and creating a work atmosphere that promotes balance. This chapter investigates how technology can be used to create equilibrium in remote work environments, with an emphasis on the tools, techniques, and practices that enable individuals to take control of their professional and personal life.

**The Double-Edged Sword of Technology**

Technology has transformed the way we work, particularly for remote workers, yet it provides both benefits and drawbacks. Understanding this dual nature is critical for effective technology use.

Benefits of Technology:

One of the most important benefits of technology for remote workers is its capacity to provide flexibility. Employees can access work-related tasks and communication tools from almost anywhere, allowing them to plan their work schedules around their personal lives. This flexibility promotes a sense of independence and control over one's time.

Improved communication tools, such as instant messaging and video conferencing, enable remote workers to collaborate and stay connected despite geographical barriers. Additionally, task management tools like Asana and Trello assist remote workers in prioritizing tasks, tracking deadlines, and managing multiple projects.

Challenges of Technology:

However, this same technology might result in overconnectivity. The ability to stay connected via email, instant messaging, or mobile apps fosters a "always-on" mentality, making it difficult for people to disconnect from work. Employees may experience burnout as a result of the blurred lines between work and home life, as they struggle to turn off notifications and recoup during their off hours.

Moreover, technology is a double-edged sword when it comes to diversions. Social media, regular notifications, and an onslaught of emails can distract remote workers from deep, concentrated work, making it difficult to maintain balance. Furthermore, information overload can leave individuals with too much material to absorb, resulting in decision fatigue and decreased productivity.

**Using Technology for Time Management**

Effective time management is critical for attaining work-life balance, particularly for remote workers who must balance personal and professional duties. Fortunately, there are several tools and tactics available to help people organize their time and be productive without sacrificing their personal life.

1. Calendar Applications.

Digital calendars, such as Google Calendar and Outlook, are wonderful tools for remote workers to plan meetings, set reminders, and set off time for focused work. These tools allow users to visualize their day and organize work in a structured manner.

Best practices:

To make calendar apps more efficient, employees can set aside separate time periods for different jobs and activities. Setting aside time for both work-related duties and personal breaks will help you maintain a balanced schedule. Setting reminders for deadlines and crucial meetings also assures that activities are finished on time, reducing last-minute anxiety.

## 2. Task Management Tools

Individuals can use applications like Trello, Asana, and Todoist to build to-do lists, prioritize activities, and track their progress. These technologies divide larger undertakings into smaller steps, making them more approachable and less overwhelming.

Best practices:

Using these methods to prioritize activities ensures that vital work is finished first, with less urgent stuff handled later. Setting deadlines and tracking progress promotes accountability and prevents workers from procrastinating.

## 3. Time-tracking software

Understanding how remote workers use their time is critical for increasing productivity. Workers can use tools like Toggl and Clockify to track how much time they spend on various tasks throughout the day. This data enables people to spot inefficiencies and manage their schedules.

Best practices:

Regularly examining time monitoring information enables remote workers to measure their productivity and change their schedules as necessary. Workers can allocate their most difficult jobs to specific times of day by recognizing productivity trends, such as the times of day when they are most concentrated.

## Accepting Communication Technology for Collaboration

Remote work necessitates excellent communication, and technology provides a variety of tools to enhance cooperation among team members, whether they live across town or over the world.

1. Instant Messaging Platforms.

Instant messaging technologies such as Slack and Microsoft Teams enable real-time collaboration, allowing for brief talks without the formality of meetings. These solutions are critical for remote workers to stay connected and communicate information effectively.

Best practices:

Creating separate channels for different projects or subjects helps to organize conversations. Setting communication conventions, such as response time guidelines, helps to keep team members from becoming overwhelmed by continual messaging.

2. Videoconferencing Tools

Zoom, Google Meet, and Microsoft Teams have become essential tools for remote workers, offering face-to-face connection in a virtual setting. Video conferencing enables for more personalized communication, which promotes team cohesion.

Best practices:

Regular video meetings are critical for sustaining team connections and ensuring everyone is in agreement. Encouraging team members to use video during meetings increases engagement and strengthens relationships.

3. Collaboration Tools.

Teams can collaborate on documents, spreadsheets, and presentations at the same time using platforms like Google Workspace and Microsoft 365. This real-time cooperation makes workflows more efficient and eliminates the need for lengthy email threads.

Best practices:

Encourage the usage of shared documents so that everyone has access to the most recent modifications. Clearly identifying roles and duties in collaborative initiatives helps to prevent confusion and promote accountability.

**Balancing Connectivity and Disconnection**

While technology improves communication and productivity, it's also critical to strike a balance between connectivity and relaxation to avoid burnout.

1. Set boundaries for work hours.

Remote workers must set clear boundaries to avoid work from interfering with leisure time. Communicating these boundaries with coworkers promotes mutual respect for work-life balance.

Best practices:

Clearly establish working hours and use calendar elements to show availability. Using "Do Not Disturb" features on messaging apps and phones during non-working hours reduces distractions.

2. Schedule technology-free downtime.

Regular pauses from technology are essential for both mental and physical wellness. Taking time away from screens allows people to recover, which improves their focus and creativity when they return to work.

Best practices:

Designating particular break periods throughout the day can assist prevent burnout. Participating in offline activities, such as exercising or spending time outside, fosters a better work-life balance.

## Leveraging Technology for Personal Well-Being

Technology can also improve personal well-being, resulting in a healthier work-life balance for remote employees.

1. Wellness Apps.

Wellness apps such as Headspace and Calm provide resources for mindfulness, meditation, and relaxation. These apps help remote workers manage stress and stay focused throughout the day.

Best practices:

Practicing mindfulness during breaks might help you relax and minimize stress. Setting daily reminders for mindfulness exercises helps to guarantee that wellness practices become ingrained in the daily routine.

2. Fitness and activity trackers.

Wearable devices and fitness apps, such as Fitbit and MyFitnessPal, let remote workers monitor their physical activity and nutrition. Staying active is critical for sustaining energy and mental clarity during the workday.

Best practices:

Setting reasonable fitness objectives promotes frequent movement and physical exercise. Joining virtual fitness challenges with coworkers can be a fun, social way to maintain health and well-being.

## Continuous Learning and Development through Technology

Technology also allows remote workers to pursue ongoing learning and professional development, which can improve personal fulfillment and work-life balance.

1. Online Learning Platforms.

Platforms such as Coursera, Udemy, and LinkedIn Learning provide hundreds of courses on a wide range of topics, allowing remote workers to learn new skills and remain competitive in their employment.

Best practices:

Allocating particular time for professional development ensures that learning is a top priority. Exploring numerous topics, especially ones unrelated to one's current position, can extend one's perspective and promote personal growth.

## 2. Networking and Community Building

Remote professionals can interact with peers, share insights, and develop support systems by using online professional networks like LinkedIn and industry-specific forums.

Best practices:

Active participation in online communities strengthens connections and promotes information sharing. Attending virtual conferences and webinars allows remote professionals to remain current on industry trends and develop their networks.

Finally, technology can help remote workers attain work-life balance. Individuals can gain control over their work and personal life by utilizing tools for time management, communication, personal well-being, and constant learning. However, it is critical to set boundaries and employ technology wisely, ensuring that it contributes rather than detracts from overall balance. With the correct strategy, remote workers can use technology to excel in their professional positions while still leading fulfilling personal lives.

# Managing Your Energy, Not Just Your Time

Many remote workers place a high value on time management in order to improve productivity. They organize tasks, meetings, and deadlines to fit into a busy daily routine, thinking that making the most of every minute is the key to success. While time management is obviously crucial, it is only one aspect of the puzzle. The capacity to manage your energy is just as crucial, if not more so. Time is limited, but energy changes throughout the day, and learning how to use it efficiently can lead to increased productivity and well-being.

This chapter will look at the notion of energy management, how it differs from time management, and practical ways for managing your energy levels as a remote worker. By focusing on when and how you invest your energy, you can not only increase performance and prevent burnout, but also establish a long-term work-life balance that fosters success.

## The Difference Between Time Management and Energy Management

Time management has long been seen as the cornerstone of productivity. It entails organising tasks to fit into a given period, with the goal of doing as much as possible within a set number of hours. While this strategy may help people become more productive, it does not account for the variations in energy and focus that everyone experiences throughout the day. This is where energy management comes in.

Unlike time management, which focuses on maximizing production under a set timetable, energy management aims to align your responsibilities with your natural energy levels. In other words, it emphasizes the timing of tasks rather than the length of time spent on them. Understanding the times of day when you are most energetic allows you to work smarter, not harder.

Key differences include:

Time Management: The primary goal is efficiency, with an emphasis on completing work within defined time frames. This strategy motivates you to get as much done as possible, regardless of how you feel physically or mentally.

Energy Management: This strategy aims to improve performance by synchronizing work with your body's natural rhythms. It enables you to execute high-energy work while your energy levels are at their height, while saving low-energy chores for times when you are less focused or tired.

By adding energy management into your daily routine, you can not only increase productivity but also maintain a healthier work-life balance.

**Understanding Your Personal Energy Cycles**

To effectively regulate your energy, you must first understand your own energy patterns. Every person has a distinct rhythm that governs their energy peaks and valleys throughout the day, which are frequently influenced by biological processes known as circadian rhythms. Circadian rhythms control many of our body's activities, including sleep-wake cycles and hormonal secretion, which influence energy levels.

Identify Your Energy Peaks:

Individuals are typically classified into three kinds based on their energy cycles:

Morning People ("Larks"): These people are most enthusiastic in the early hours of the day, peaking between 8 a.m. and 12 p.m. If you fall into this category, schedule your most demanding responsibilities, such as deep work or problem solving, for the morning.

Night Owls: People in this category tend to have more energy later in the day, resulting in an increase in productivity in the late afternoon or evening. If you are more concentrated during these hours, postpone your complex work until later in the day.

Midday Peaks: Many people get surges of energy around mid-morning or early afternoon. If your energy levels change throughout the day, it's critical to note these moments so that you can plan your work properly.

Tracking your energy levels:

Spend a few days measuring your energy levels at various times of day to obtain a better grasp of them. Every hour, score your focus and energy on a 1-10 scale. After a few days, you should see patterns in your energy peaks and drops. This information will help you structure your weekday so that tasks coincide with your natural energy patterns.

**Task Alignment and Energy Levels**

Once you've found your energy peaks, the next step is to plan your duties around these fluctuations. The idea is to assign high-focus activities while your energy is at its peak and low-focus chores when you are naturally less energized.

High-energy tasks:

These tasks need significant concentration and mental effort. Examples include:

- Problem-solving
- Creative brainstorming
- Complex decision-making.
- Deep work, such as programming, writing, or designing

If you know you have a peak energy window between 9 a.m. and 11 a.m., now is the time to handle these high-energy tasks. Completing tasks while you are most aware allows you to give them your undivided attention and produce high-quality outcomes.

Low Energy Tasks:

These are chores that demand less concentration and can be accomplished even when you're exhausted. Examples include:

- Answering emails
- Administrative tasks.
- Filing, Data Entry, or Paperwork
- Organize your workspace

It's ideal to switch to these usual duties when you're feeling low energy, which could be after lunch or at the end of the day. They do not demand much cognitive effort, allowing you to make progress without draining your energy reserves.

By matching your responsibilities to your energy levels, you'll operate more efficiently and lower your chances of burnout.

**Managing Breaks to Replenish Energy**

Taking regular breaks is essential for maintaining energy levels throughout the day. According to research, working for lengthy periods of time without taking a break causes weariness and reduces productivity. Breaks, on the other hand, provide your brain time to rest and regroup, allowing you to sustain focus throughout time.

Effective Break Strategies:

The Pomodoro Technique is a famous strategy in which you work for 25 minutes and then take a 5-minute break. After four work sessions, you take a 15-30 minute break. This systematic technique allows you to stay focused without overworking your brain.

90-Minute Work Cycles: According to the Ultradian Rhythm, our brains perform best in 90-minute cycles. After 90 minutes of serious work, take a 15- to 20-minute break to rejuvenate.

Movement Breaks: Incorporate physical movement into your breaks, such as a short stroll or stretching. Movement improves circulation and energizes both the body and the mind, allowing you to return to work with renewed vitality.

Mindfulness during breaks:

Mindfulness methods like as meditation, deep breathing, or simply relaxing during breaks can improve brain clarity and reduce stress. These little moments of mindfulness allow you to reboot mentally, making it simpler to stay focused and enthusiastic throughout the day.

**Nutrition and Energy Management**

Your nutrition has a huge impact on how you feel during the day. Eating the appropriate foods at the right times can help you stay energized and focused, whereas bad dietary choices can cause energy dips and decreased productivity.

Foods that boost energy:

Complex Carbohydrates: Whole grains, fruits, and vegetables release glucose into your circulation on a consistent basis, providing you with long-term energy.

Proteins: Lean meats, nuts, and legumes help you maintain attention and stamina, which supports brain function over long periods of time.

Healthy Fats: Foods like avocados, almonds, and seeds provide long-lasting energy since they digest slowly and provide consistent fuel for your body and brain.

Avoiding Foods That Drain Your Energy:

Sugary foods and caffeine overloads may provide a temporary burst of energy, but they frequently lead to collapses later. Limit your intake of these foods and instead choose balanced meals and snacks that provide long-lasting energy.

Hydration:

Staying hydrated is critical for sustaining energy and concentration. Even minor dehydration can cause weariness and lower cognitive performance. Drink plenty of water throughout the day to keep alert and energized.

**Sleep and Its Role in Energy Management**

Sleep is likely the most essential component in determining energy levels. Without adequate rest, it is practically hard to retain focus and productivity. Poor sleep also causes irritation, decreased decision-making, and an increased risk of burnout.

Sleep Hygiene Tips:

Maintain a Consistent Schedule: Going to bed and getting up at the same time every day, including weekends, helps regulate your body's internal clock, making it easier to fall asleep and wake up feeling refreshed.

Create a Relaxing Environment: Make sure your bedroom is cool, dark, and silent. Reduce screen time at least an hour before bedtime, as blue light from electronic devices can interfere with your ability to fall asleep.

For example, you could read, stretch lightly, or meditate. This indicates to your body that it's time to relax and prepares you for a good night's sleep.

By putting sleep first, you'll wake up with more energy and be better prepared to handle your task throughout the day.

**Using Technology to Manage Energy**

When used properly, technology may be a valuable asset in energy management. A variety of apps and tools are available to help you track your energy levels, manage breaks, and optimize your work schedule.

Energy Boosting Tools:

Focus@Will: This app provides scientifically crafted music to help you focus and stay energized throughout work sessions.

Be Focused: Based on the Pomodoro Technique, this tool allows you to work in intervals and reminds you to take frequent rests.

Sleep Cycle: This software monitors your sleep habits and helps you get up during your lightest sleep period, allowing you to start the day feeling energized.

Incorporating these techniques into your daily routine will help you regulate your energy levels, avoid burnout, and increase overall productivity. By using technology to monitor your energy levels, you may create a work environment that promotes your mental and physical well-being.

Use Technology Wisely:

While technology provides numerous tools to assist with energy management, it is critical to use these tools responsibly. Overreliance on electronics, particularly when multitasking, can result in distractions and mental weariness. Make sure you use technology to boost your productivity rather than harm it. Set clear screen time limits and avoid falling into the temptation of constant connectedness, which can drain your energy over time. For example, try turning off non-essential alerts during intense work sessions and using applications like Focus@Will or Be Focused to create regular work times that allow you to concentrate without distractions.

Finally, managing your energy, rather than just your time, is the key to maintaining a healthy work-life balance as a remote worker. While time management helps you plan your day's duties, energy management enables you to operate more efficiently by aligning those tasks with your natural cycles. This method not only boosts productivity but also promotes mental and physical well-being, lowering the danger of burnout and assisting you in achieving long-term success in both your professional and personal life.

You can improve your everyday performance by recognizing your personal energy cycles, aligning work with your energy levels, and taking regular recharge pauses. Furthermore, being attentive of your diet, hydration, and sleep patterns ensures that you have the energy to meet the demands of your job without jeopardizing your health. With the correct tools and tactics, remote workers may master energy management and live a more balanced, joyful, and productive existence.

Rather than cramming as much as possible into your calendar, try to optimize when and how you complete things based on your energy level. This holistic approach ensures that you not only get things done but also have the energy to enjoy life outside of work. Remote workers that implement energy management methods will be more productive, satisfied, and less stressed, laying the groundwork for long-term success.

By embracing the power of energy management, you can change the way you work and live, making productivity a long-term achievement rather than a temporary ambition.

# The Importance of Flexibility

Flexibility has emerged as one of the most important characteristics of successfully managing remote work. Unlike traditional office workplaces, where hours are generally rigid and employees must perform within defined constraints, remote work provides a unique chance to adjust schedules and duties to individual needs, preferences, and personal responsibilities. True flexibility, however, is more than just changing work hours; it is about developing a mindset and a work structure that allows for adaptability, responsiveness, and balance. Flexibility allows you to manage the unpredictable parts of your career and personal life. This chapter looks at why flexibility is important for remote workers, how to apply it effectively, and the numerous personal and professional benefits it provides.

## Why Flexibility Matters in Remote Work

Flexibility is critical in helping remote workers manage their time, energy, and task more effectively. The option to select when and where to work is a big advantage, but it also necessitates discipline, planning, and the capacity to adjust to continual change. Remote employment requires more self-management and flexibility than regular office settings. In an age where work-life balance is becoming increasingly important, flexibility allows remote workers to effortlessly merge professional responsibilities with personal demands, resulting in a harmonic combination that is sometimes impossible to achieve in a conventional, office-bound routine.

One of the primary benefits of flexibility is the capacity to manage personal commitments while maintaining job performance. Remote workers can better combine family care, household management, and even personal growth, providing for a more fulfilling existence outside of work. Whether it's attending to a child's needs, scheduling doctor's visits, or simply taking time to recharge, flexibility enables employees to maintain high performance while still meeting life's unavoidable demands.

Furthermore, flexibility improves productivity by allowing employees to complete activities during their peak productivity hours. Rather of adhering to a traditional 9-to-5 workweek, remote workers can time their duties around peak energy hours, ensuring that they work when they are most awake and focused. This tailored approach to time management results in better outcomes and more efficient use of time, which promotes job satisfaction and a sense of success.

In addition to enhancing productivity, flexibility can help to minimize stress and burnout. Remote workers are frequently at danger of overworking since the line between personal and professional life blurs. However, when correctly managed, a flexible schedule allows for frequent pauses, mental resets, and time for self-care, all of which are critical for long-term well-being. Flexibility helps workers avoid burnout by giving them greater discretion over how, when, and where they work, allowing them to rest and recover.

Flexibility also provides remote workers with the agility required to respond to unforeseen circumstances. Whether it's an urgent family concern or an unexpected business assignment, the ability to transfer projects and alter calendars on the fly means that both professional and personal priorities are handled with minimal stress. This adaptability provides a higher sense of control, reduces worry, and promotes a more favorable work-life balance.

**Types of Flexibility in Remote Work**

Flexibility in remote work takes several forms, each of which plays an important part in creating a sustainable and effective work environment. Understanding the various sorts of flexibility is critical for successfully incorporating them into your work routine.

1. Flexible working hours (time flexibility)

One of the most frequently mentioned advantages of remote work is increased time flexibility. Flexible work hours, as opposed to the usual 9-to-5 schedule, allow you to start and end your day when it is most convenient for you. This could entail starting sooner or later than usual office hours, or perhaps dividing tasks across different sections of the day. For example, some employees may discover that they are most productive in the early mornings, but others thrive in the evenings. This type of flexibility enables employees to plan their days around their peak productivity times, allowing them to create high-quality work without having to force their energy levels to conform to a rigid timetable.

The advantages of time flexibility are numerous. It not only allows for better management of personal responsibilities, such as family obligations or health appointments, but it also increases productivity by scheduling professional assignments during peak energy periods. This leads to more efficient work and less time spent because remote workers can work smarter rather than harder.

2. Flexible Work Locations

Remote work reduces the necessity for employees to be physically present in an office, giving them the option to work anywhere they wish. Location flexibility allows for a change of atmosphere, which can promote creativity, eliminate monotony, and increase job satisfaction. The capacity to establish an ideal work environment, whether it is quiet seclusion at home or a more lively setting in a café, can significantly improve focus and productivity.

The benefits of location flexibility go beyond avoiding the daily commute. Working from a place that meets your needs reduces the stress associated with traditional office environments, resulting in a more comfortable and productive workday.

Furthermore, the lack of a commute saves time and energy, allowing remote workers to better utilize these resources in both their professional and personal life.

3. Flexibility in Task Management

Task management flexibility entails the ability to choose not just when and where to work, but also how to handle tasks. This type of flexibility is especially vital in remote work, where individuals are generally responsible for managing workloads. Task management flexibility allows remote workers to prioritize tasks based on their energy levels, deadlines, and personal preferences, ensuring that high-priority tasks are accomplished when they are most productive.

For example, some jobs may require intense concentration and should be accomplished in one sitting, whilst others may be better spread out throughout the day. The capacity to structure your workload in a way that makes sense to you can result in a higher sense of ownership over your job, less stress, and better performance.

### The Advantages of Flexibility in Work-Life Balance

One of the fundamental reasons why remote workers require flexibility is to maintain a healthy work-life balance. Without the tight structures of traditional office environments, remote workers can choose a work schedule that fits into their overall life, rather than forcing life to fit around work. This makes the distinction between personal and professional commitments more fluid and manageable, preventing one from dominating the other.

One of the primary advantages of flexibility in this regard is a reduction in friction between work and personal life. Remote workers can handle personal responsibilities, such as running errands or picking up children from school, without jeopardizing professional productivity. This capacity to manage personal duties in a way that complements rather than competes with work can result in significant stress reduction and an overall higher quality of life.

Flexibility not only reduces work-life friction, but it also helps to improve mental health and well-being. Having control over one's schedule can alleviate stress, anxiety, and increase job satisfaction. Remote workers who can manage their time well typically report feeling more fulfilled both professionally and emotionally, since they may establish a lifestyle that promotes their mental and emotional health.

Flexibility develops an environment that promotes creativity and innovation. The ability to take pauses as needed, work from multiple locations, and move away from projects when energy levels are low helps the mind to rest and recharge. This mental break frequently leads to more creative solutions and new views, making flexibility an effective tool not only for increasing productivity but also for promoting innovation.

**Strategies for Adding Flexibility to Your Work Routine**

While flexibility has many advantages, it must be used intelligently to ensure that it fulfills your professional and personal needs. The successful deployment of flexibility necessitates a balance between structure and freedom. Here are a few tips to make flexibility a useful and effective component of your remote work schedule:

1. Establish clear expectations with your team.

Even if your schedule is flexible, it's critical to communicate clear boundaries and objectives with your team or management. Transparency regarding your availability for meetings, task deadlines, and communication ensures that flexibility does not jeopardize teamwork or project timeframes. Setting these expectations promotes trust and ensures that everyone agrees on how and when work will be completed.

2. Develop a Flexible, Yet Structured Routine.

Flexibility does not imply the absence of structure. In fact, too much freedom without a set pattern can result in chaos, procrastination, and stress. To make the most of flexibility, develop a defined daily routine that allows for alterations as needed. For example, you may set core work hours but allow for flexibility surrounding meetings, breaks, and personal responsibilities. This blend of structure and independence guarantees that you remain productive while still benefiting from the flexibility that remote work provides.

3. Prioritize tasks according to energy levels.

One of the most effective methods to maximize the benefits of flexibility is to schedule your most critical work around your natural energy peaks. Determine when you are most awake and concentrated throughout the day, and set aside those times for high-priority tasks that need intense concentration. Save less taxing duties, such as responding to emails, for times when your energy is naturally low.

4. Use Technology to Support Flexibility.

Use the variety of technology solutions available to enable a flexible work schedule. Time-tracking apps can help you keep on track with your work hours, but project management software can ensure that you fulfill deadlines even if your working hours change from day to day. Communication systems can also help you stay connected to your team, ensuring that flexibility does not come at the expense of collaboration.

**Overcoming the Challenges of Flexibility**

While flexibility has many benefits, it can often provide issues. One of the most common is staying disciplined. Without a strict workplace structure, it is easy to postpone or let work spill into personal time. However, there are techniques for overcoming these obstacles and ensuring that flexibility results in increased productivity rather than distractions.

1. Maintaining boundaries.

It is critical to set clear boundaries between work and personal life. Even with a flexible schedule, establishing distinct work hours might help keep work from intruding into personal time. Avoid checking emails or completing activities outside of these hours unless absolutely required. Creating physical boundaries, such as a designated workstation, can also serve to reinforce the distinction between work and personal life.

2. Preventing Overwork

Flexibility should prevent burnout, not exacerbate it. Remote workers are especially vulnerable to overwork since they are frequently pressured to be ready at all times. To avoid this, schedule regular breaks throughout the day and restrict your work hours so you have time to refuel. Making time for yourself is just as vital as getting work done.

3. Staying Organized

Staying organized is crucial for remote workers because they lack the external structure that an office offers. Task management tools, calendars, and to-do lists can help you stay on top of priorities and deadlines. The organization guarantees that flexibility does not result in missed deadlines or increased stress.

## The Role of Employers in Supporting Flexibility

Flexibility benefits both individuals and companies, as it can lead to better productivity, job satisfaction, and staff retention. However, for flexibility to be effective and durable, leadership must provide active support. Employers have a critical role in fostering an environment that encourages and manages flexible work for all team members.

One of the most important ways organizations can encourage flexibility is to offer flexible hours and remote work choices. Employers can promote a results-oriented culture that favors production over adherence to typical work schedules by focusing on the quality of the work workers produce rather than when and where they work. This mentality shift allows employees to take responsibility of their jobs and work in ways that best meet their unique needs, resulting in increased productivity and morale.

Employers can also provide tools and resources that allow for flexible work arrangements. Providing access to communication platforms, project management software, and collaborative tools ensures that teams stay connected and productive no matter where or when they work. These services help to avoid the isolation and disorganization that can sometimes accompany flexible work arrangements.

Beyond offering tools, organizations may foster a culture that actively encourages and respects flexibility. This involves recognizing the value of work-life balance and encouraging people to take the necessary breaks to recover. Employers who encourage open communication, trust their employees to manage their schedules responsibly, and model flexibility among their leadership teams establish a strong example for their employees.

Finally, businesses can provide training on time management, productivity tactics, and mental health support to help employees overcome the obstacles that come with flexible employment. This investment in employee well-being promotes flexibility while also ensuring that employees have the necessary skills and tools to flourish in a remote work environment.

In today's increasingly digital and remote work environment, flexibility has become critical to long-term success and well-being. It enables employees to create a work regimen that complements their lifestyle, promotes balance, and increases productivity. Remote workers can establish a personalized approach that benefits both their professional and personal life by embracing several sorts of flexibility, such as time, location, and task management.

To guarantee that flexibility works for you, you must exercise discipline, set clear boundaries, and implement it thoughtfully. With the appropriate strategies in place, flexibility allows employees to thrive, handle their obligations with ease, and achieve the elusive balance of personal and professional success. Employers play an important role in promoting this balance by offering the appropriate tools, resources, and motivation to make flexibility a part of their company culture.

Finally, flexibility gives the freedom required to not just survive, but thrive in remote work environments. It allows remote workers to customize their workweek to meet their own demands, boost long-term well-being, and increase overall productivity. Remote workers can achieve a long-term and meaningful work-life balance by embracing and utilizing flexibility.

# Burnout Prevention for Remote Workers

Burnout has become a major worry among remote workers, owing to the difficulties of separating professional and home lives. As the line between home and work blurs, many remote employees find themselves working longer hours, dealing with constant distractions, and feeling isolated. Together, these concerns form a perfect storm for burnout—a state of mental, physical, and emotional tiredness that jeopardizes both well-being and productivity. In this chapter, we'll look at what burnout is, why it's become so common in remote work contexts, and how to spot and prevent it. By learning to detect the symptoms and implementing healthy work practices, remote workers may safeguard their well-being and sustain productivity, enjoying the unique benefits of remote work without becoming victims.

## What is Burnout?

Burnout is a state of chronic stress that causes emotional, mental, and physical depletion. It frequently develops gradually when the demands of job outweigh an individual's ability to cope over time. This cumulative stress can cause separation from work, lower productivity, and, in severe situations, mental health issues such as anxiety and depression. Some common burnout symptoms include weariness that lasts even after resting, a developing detachment or cynicism toward work, and a loss in performance, despite working more hours. Remote workers confront special obstacles in diagnosing burnout since they do not have regular, face-to-face connection with coworkers, making early warning signs tougher to spot. This isolation may foster a "always-on" mentality in which employees feel compelled to be constantly logged in, hastening the onset of burnout.

**Causes of Burnout in Remote Work.**

Burnout can develop gradually, particularly in remote work environments where the causes may go unreported. One major factor is a lack of separation between work and personal life. Remote employment frequently blurs the distinction between these two spheres, making it easy for business to flow over into personal life. Without a dedicated office or set working hours, remote workers may find themselves checking emails after hours, skipping breaks, or working late into the evening on a continuous basis. This absence of boundaries encourages overwork, ultimately leading to burnout.

Isolation and loneliness can also lead to burnout in remote work. While remote work provides freedom, it misses the social features of typical offices, where casual discussions and face-to-face encounters with coworkers contribute to a sense of community and belonging. Without these regular connections, distant workers may feel isolated, which can affect motivation and contribute to stress. This solitude is exacerbated by an intensified need to perform. Many remote employees feel compelled to "prove" their productivity, frequently by working extended hours or replying to communications immediately. This pressure generates a cycle of perpetual availability, leaving little time for relaxation and rehabilitation and pushing workers toward burnout.

Another major obstacle for remote workers is juggling work and household duties. Working from home frequently requires managing business work with personal distractions such as family members, housemates, or household chores. This continual switching between tasks causes mental weariness, making it difficult to remain focused and productive. Finally, a lack of routine may contribute to burnout. A scheduled schedule promotes a sense of normalcy, but remote work can lead to irregular work hours or disregard of breaks, resulting in disorganization and overwhelm, which contributes to stress.

**Recognizing the Early Warning Signs of Burnout**

Being able to recognize burnout early is critical for controlling it before it gets unmanageable. Persistent fatigue is one of the first indicators, since you feel fatigued and depleted even after a full night's sleep. Irritability and frustration may also grow, making you more sensitive or reactive to workplace obstacles or interactions with coworkers. A steady drop in motivation can occur, where things that were once enjoyable or intriguing begin to feel like a burden. Furthermore, difficulty concentrating becomes more common, making it harder to remain focused or remember critical activities. Another indicator is withdrawal from social connections; some people may begin to avoid interacting with friends, family, or colleagues as a coping tactic. Recognizing these symptoms early on allows you to take proactive steps to prevent burnout from worsening.

**Strategies for Burnout Prevention**

Preventing burnout requires a proactive approach that prioritizes balance, rest, and personal well-being. One of the most effective ways is to set clear boundaries between work and personal life. Setting specified work hours and designating a specialized workstation might help you create this distinction, allowing you to mentally "switch off" after your job is complete. Setting limits can help prevent work from taking up personal time and lessen feelings of overwork.

Taking regular pauses throughout the day is also important for preventing burnout. Working for long periods of time without rest can deplete mental energy, making you more prone to weariness. Adopting practices such as the Pomodoro Technique, which involves working in focused intervals followed by brief pauses, can help you stay focused and avoid mental tiredness. Taking a short stroll during breaks or leaving your desk for meals might also help to freshen your thoughts and increase productivity.

Developing a disciplined schedule is another helpful method for avoiding burnout. Having a routine provides a sense of control and organization, which reduces feelings of overwhelm. Starting the day with a morning ritual that mentally prepares you for work might help to set a pleasant tone. Planning chores the night before or at the start of the day allows you to approach work with a clear understanding of what needs to be done, preventing you from feeling overwhelmed by an unstructured workload.

Staying in touch with coworkers and friends helps prevent isolation, which is a big factor to burnout in remote work. Schedule virtual coffee breaks or team meetings to provide the social interaction and support that many remote workers lack. Participating in online forums or professional groups also provides networking possibilities and a common space to discuss issues and celebrate accomplishments, which fosters a sense of belonging.

Managing your workload and setting reasonable goals is another important burnout prevention method. Remote workers can easily overcommit or take on too many duties. Breaking down major projects into smaller, more manageable steps and setting clear, quantifiable goals for each day or week can help avoid work from becoming overwhelming. It is also critical to identify when you are at capacity and to feel comfortable declining extra duties if necessary.

Prioritizing self-care is essential for preserving both mental and physical wellness. Incorporating physical activity into your daily routine, whether through yoga, walking, or a gym, can help you relax and focus. Mindfulness or meditation can also help you stay focused, reduce stress, and build resilience to burnout. Getting enough sleep and eating a nutritious food are two equally vital components of self-care that benefit both your body and mind.

**The Role of Employers in Preventing Burnout**

Employers have an important role in minimizing burnout among remote employees. A supportive work culture that encourages work-life balance can have an impact. Employers can promote a healthy balance by creating a culture in which taking regular breaks and time off is valued, so ensuring that workloads remain manageable. Providing mental health resources, such as counseling or wellness programs, demonstrates to employees that their well-being is important and that they will be supported if they feel stress or burnout. Companies may foster a culture in which remote workers feel encouraged and empowered to preserve their well-being by setting realistic expectations and valuing their personal time.

## Technology and Tools for Burnout Prevention

Remote workers can use various apps and tools to manage their workload and stress levels. Time-tracking tools, such as Toggl or Clockify, allow you to track your time across many projects, making it easier to spot and avoid overworking. Wellness applications like Headspace and Calm offer guided meditation and mindfulness activities that can help reduce stress and enhance mental clarity. Project management solutions such as Asana and Trello keep tasks organized and reasonable, allowing remote workers to stay on top of their obligations without feeling overwhelmed.

Burnout does not have to be an unavoidable consequence of remote employment. Remote workers can enjoy the convenience of working from home without jeopardizing their health by detecting warning signs, applying effective techniques, and balancing work and personal life. Setting limits, keeping social relationships, prioritizing self-care, and using productivity tools can help to prevent burnout. With the correct attitude and mindset, remote work can be both productive and satisfying, allowing you to excel in your profession while maintaining your health and motivation in the long run.

# Creating a Work-Life Integration Strategy

Work-life integration is about balancing professional and personal commitments in a way that benefits both areas, rather than striving for full separation. Unlike work-life balance, which implies an equal division, work-life integration allows for a more fluid transition between professional and personal activities. This method is especially useful for remote workers, as the lines between work and home frequently blur. In this chapter, we'll look at the concept of work-life integration, its benefits, and how to create a strategy that works for your specific scenario. By adopting this approach, you can increase productivity at work while also nourishing your personal well-being.

## Understanding Work-Life Integration

Work-life integration is a strategy that permits professional and personal duties to coexist without strict boundaries. Instead of aiming to devote equal time to each areas, this technique emphasizes combining them in a way that fits your lifestyle. For remote workers, whose job frequently takes place in the same environment as their personal lives, integration can feel more practical than rigorous separation. For example, you could work a few hours in the morning, then attend to family responsibilities in the afternoon before returning to work later in the evening. This flexibility allows you to fit work around your life's demands rather than sacrificing one for the other.

The primary distinction between work-life balance and work-life integration is how each approaches the relationship between work and personal life. Work-life balance emphasizes keeping these aspects separate, with a clear line between work and personal time. Work-life integration, on the other hand, involves blending work and personal tasks, allowing for smoother transitions between the two. This approach can be especially effective for remote workers, who often have less rigid boundaries than those working in a traditional office setting.

**The Benefits of Work-Life Integration**

Work-life integration has various advantages, particularly for remote workers who frequently experience blurred borders between their professional and personal lives. One big advantage is more flexibility, which allows you to better manage your time by balancing professional and personal obligations, and vice versa. For example, you could attend a child's school event during the day and then catch up on work in the evening. This flexibility lessens the guilt associated with taking time off for personal reasons, as long as work commitments are completed.

Another advantage is lower stress. Work-life integration reduces the stress that frequently comes with attempting to achieve a strict split by allowing personal and professional life to coexist. You're less likely to feel guilty about dealing with personal issues during the workday or, conversely, focused on work when you have other responsibilities, which might help you maintain your mental health.

Work-life integration often results in increased productivity. The strategy allows you to match job tasks to your natural energy levels. If you are more productive in the mornings, you can devote that time to more difficult work, saving less demanding chores for the afternoon. This ability to work while you're at your peak performance can help you maximize production while maintaining quality.

Work-life integration increases life happiness by encouraging a more holistic lifestyle that meets both personal and professional requirements. Rather than feeling pulled between work and personal life, this technique allows you to handle both areas harmoniously, resulting in a sense of accomplishment and well-being.

**Develop a Work-Life Integration Strategy**

A good work-life integration strategy demands careful planning. Begin by reviewing your priorities—identify the most critical duties in both your professional and personal life. Understanding what is most important to you in each area can allow you to better spend your time. Make a list of your job assignments and deadlines, as well as important personal commitments, and prioritize them according to deadlines, energy levels, and long-term goals.

Once you've established your priorities, create a flexible timetable that includes both business and personal responsibilities. Use time-blocking tactics to set aside particular times for work, personal pursuits, and downtime. Being willing to change your schedule as needed might help you adapt to new priorities or unforeseen demands while maintaining productivity and personal well-being.

While work-life integration promotes flexibility, it is nevertheless vital to set boundaries. This will help to keep work from taking over your personal life, and vice versa. Set aside times during the day when you are not available for business, such as family dinners or workout sessions, and discuss these boundaries with your team or management so that they respect your personal time.

Technology can be an effective tool for work-life integration, particularly for remote employees. Use productivity applications like Trello or Asana to keep track of job assignments and deadlines. Setting reminders for both business and personal commitments might help you stay on top of your tasks without feeling overwhelmed.

Finally, regular breaks and relaxation are vital for sustaining energy and avoiding burnout. Regular breaks can take many forms, such as going outside for a short walk, eating lunch away from your workplace, or stretching for a few minutes. Make careful to schedule lengthier periods of rest, such as weekends or vacations, when you may completely detach from work. This time to recharge promotes long-term productivity and minimizes mental and physical exhaustion caused by continually being in "work mode."

## Common Challenges in Work-Life Integration

While work-life integration has numerous advantages, it is not without obstacles. Remote workers, in particular, may encounter unique challenges that make this strategy challenging. One of the most typical difficulties is overlapping roles. Without defined boundaries, work responsibilities can easily bleed into personal time, and vice versa. For example, you may find yourself reading work emails during family dinners or performing household chores while on a work call. To overcome this, utilize time-blocking to build an organized timetable that balances work and personal responsibilities. Set strict boundaries during key times, such as family gatherings or working on a deadline, to reduce overlap.

Another common difficulty for remote workers is a lack of organization. Flexibility without structure can lead to disorder, which reduces productivity. Without a fixed pattern, some remote workers may become overwhelmed by juggling too many obligations at once. To address this, create a daily regimen that balances flexibility and structure. Having a plan for both your professional and personal activities ensures that nothing slips through the cracks, which can reduce stress and promote work-life balance.

Disconnecting from work is another prevalent obstacle in a remote work setting. When work and personal life overlap, it can be difficult to "switch off," resulting in overwork and, eventually, burnout. To combat this, establish and adhere to specific work hours. At the end of your workday, try turning off your computer or creating a ritual to signify the start of personal time. A defined workstation, if possible, can also help to establish physical boundaries between work and home, making it simpler to disconnect at the end of each day.

**Measuring the effectiveness of your work-life integration**

After executing your work-life integration strategy, it's critical to evaluate its performance and make changes as needed. Signs that your strategy is working include an increased sense of job satisfaction, which allows you to complete duties efficiently and without feeling overwhelmed. Furthermore, if your personal life is meaningful, with time for self-care, interests, and relationships, your integration approach is most likely balanced and beneficial to your well-being.

Energy levels are another useful sign. If you are continuously exhausted, it could be a symptom that your job and personal lives aren't as harmonious as they could be. Balanced energy levels, in which you feel recharged and capable of tackling both professional and personal responsibilities, indicate a good work-life integration plan. If any of these areas are lacking, consider making changes to ensure that your professional and personal demands are satisfied in a sustainable manner.

## The Role of Employers in Work-Life Integration

Employers may help remote workers integrate their work and personal lives by providing them with the necessary tools, flexibility, and understanding. Employers can help by giving flexible work hours, which allow employees to balance personal and professional duties. Access to enabling technology, like as communication platforms and project management software, is particularly critical since these tools help staff keep organized and engaged.

Employers can also help with work-life integration by encouraging employees to take time off. Employers can assist prevent burnout and increase long-term productivity by developing a working culture that values breaks and vacation time. Employees who feel encouraged in merging work and personal lives are more likely to stay motivated, productive, and loyal to the firm.

Work-life integration is about striking a balance between your professional and personal commitments, rather than viewing them as separate, conflicting areas of your life. By reviewing your priorities, defining boundaries, and utilizing flexible scheduling, you may develop a strategy that supports both areas in a balanced and fulfilling manner. While obstacles may arise, remaining adaptable and continually analyzing your strategy will help you maintain a balanced, rewarding remote work experience. Work-life integration allows you to enjoy the freedom of remote work while also cultivating your personal well-being, resulting in a lifestyle that is fulfilling in both professional and personal worlds.

# The Importance of Saying No

One of the most difficult but necessary talents in the world of remote work is the ability to say "no." In a virtual setting where the lines between business and personal life are frequently blurred, it's easy to feel compelled to take on more responsibilities or commit to more than you can handle. However, repeatedly answering "yes" to every request can rapidly result in fatigue, tension, and decreased productivity. To prosper in a remote work environment, it is critical to grasp why saying no is important, recognize its benefits, and adopt practical techniques for incorporating this ability into daily life.

Saying no can be difficult due to cultural expectations, fear of failing others, and a desire to be perceived as trustworthy and helpful. Many people have feelings of guilt when they deny a request, particularly in professional contexts where they wish to be viewed as valuable team members. This is especially true for remote workers, who may feel compelled to justify their hard work by agreeing to every task assigned to them. There are several reasons for this hesitation. The fear of losing out is a typical cause; many people are concerned that saying no will prohibit them from pursuing lucrative job opportunities or promotion opportunities. There's also the natural desire to please others, when people feel obligated to help and may feel guilty if they refuse a request. Additionally, individuals may be concerned that declining new responsibilities will make them appear unable or reluctant to contribute.

Understanding these considerations is the first step in overcoming the reluctance to say no. Recognizing that this hesitation is typical can make remote workers feel less alone in their struggles. Furthermore, by identifying the exact causes of this difficulty, it becomes easier to address them immediately and start building better limits.

While saying no might be tough, doing it wisely can have a big positive impact on both professional and personal outcomes. One of the key benefits is increased productivity. When you agree to every task, your burden expands exponentially, reducing your concentration on high-priority obligations. Mastering the art of saying no allows you to focus on tasks that are more relevant to your goals and have a greater impact on your work performance. Focusing on key work rather than juggling multiple requests can dramatically increase productivity.

Another significant benefit is improved work-life balance. Maintaining personal time might be difficult for remote professionals who must frequently balance home and business responsibilities. Turning down non-essential requests frees up time for relaxation, family, and other personal pursuits. This distinction is essential for maintaining mental health and preventing you from feeling always "on the clock." Furthermore, declining superfluous obligations or scheduling meeting times helps establish clear work-life boundaries, which is especially important in a remote work environment where physical separation between work and home life may not exist.

Learning to say no also has significant benefits in terms of stress reduction and burnout. Overcommitment frequently results in feelings of overwhelm and stress, which can eventually lead to burnout. When you deny extra obligations that exceed your capabilities, you keep your burden modest and protect your well-being. This technique not only helps you maintain your mental and emotional health, but it also enables you to produce higher-quality work on the projects you choose to prioritize.

Ironically, saying no can boost respect from coworkers and managers. Setting boundaries, when done intelligently, demonstrates that you respect your time and are devoted to generating high-quality work rather than overworking yourself. Colleagues and managers frequently value employees who are selective in their commitments because it indicates professionalism, self-awareness, and a focus on high-impact contributions.

Mastering the ability to say no involves practice and strategy. It is critical to approach this skill cautiously to ensure that denying requests does not ruin relationships or cause guilt. A pleasant and respectful demeanor is one excellent strategy. Saying no does not have to be abrupt or dismissive; expressing gratitude for the opportunity and providing a clear yet precise rationale for declining can help you keep a strong relationship with the individual making the request. For example, saying "I appreciate you thinking of me" or "Thank you for considering me for this task" establishes a courteous tone and shows that you value the request, even if you are unable to accomplish it.

Another useful strategy is to provide alternatives, which demonstrates a willingness to contribute in a different role or assist in the resolution of a problem. For example, you may suggest another coworker who has the time to help or volunteer to return the assignment later when your calendar is less hectic. This method offers a solution-oriented answer, highlighting that your refusal is due to existing capacity rather than a lack of desire to support the team.

Another method is to understand your limitations. Before accepting to a new duty, consider your present workload and personal responsibilities. Understanding your limitations enables you to make informed judgments about whether you can take on more work without sacrificing quality or well-being. Reviewing your to-do list and determining a maximum number of tasks or hours per day will help you set realistic boundaries and avoid overcommitment.

The "Yes, But" approach is also useful in instances where a direct no would appear too harsh or confrontational. You can meet some of the expectations without overextending yourself by agreeing to a portion of the request but placing clear limitations on your engagement. For example, you could agree to join in a brainstorming session but state that you will be unable to lead the entire project owing to other responsibilities. This compromise can enable you contribute substantially while remaining within your constraints.

Mastering the art of saying no is especially important for remote workers due to the specific problems that virtual work settings present. Remote workers frequently feel pressured to be continually available, responding to messages and requests outside of business hours. By declining after-hours duties and unneeded meetings, remote employees can protect their personal time and prevent the "always-on" mentality, which can quickly lead to tiredness. Additionally, saying no to non-urgent activities or unproductive meetings allows remote workers to focus on high-priority assignments despite the possible distractions of working from home.

The emotional obstacles of saying no should not be underestimated, as many remote workers feel guilty or fearful when they decline jobs, especially if they are concerned about job security or perceived reliability. It is critical to rethink this perspective and recognize that saying no does not lessen your value as a team member. In many circumstances, imposing boundaries demonstrates that you care about your efforts and are committed to producing high-quality results. Reframing a "no" as a strategy to protect your ability to perform well on critical duties can help relieve guilt and underline that saying no is a professional, good decision.

Accepting the power of saying no is a critical step for remote workers seeking to safeguard their time, maintain a good work-life balance, and avoid burnout. You can learn to say no without guilt or fear by setting clear boundaries, using respectful refusal strategies, and developing self-awareness. This creates the necessary room to focus on what is genuinely important, reduces stress, and leads to better outcomes both professionally and personally. Finally, saying no means taking control of your time and energy, allowing you to contribute effectively and achieve success in a remote work setting.

# Mental Health and Self-Care in Remote Work

Remote work has increased at an exponential rate in recent years, providing employees with hitherto unattainable levels of freedom and autonomy. However, the change to working from home presents unique problems that can have a substantial impact on mental health. Without the clear limits of a regular office environment, remote workers frequently endure increased stress, loneliness, and burnout. In this chapter, we will look at the specific mental health difficulties that remote workers experience and offer practical solutions for maintaining mental health and incorporating self-care into everyday routines.

Understanding the Mental Health Challenges of Remote Work

Working from home presents unique problems that can have a negative impact on mental health. Key variables like as isolation, blurred work-life boundaries, and a lack of structure contribute to an atmosphere in which remote workers may struggle to maintain their emotional well-being.

Isolation is one of the most serious mental health concerns that remote workers encounter. In a traditional office setting, everyday face-to-face contacts with coworkers foster social connection, teamwork, and camaraderie. However, in a distant context, these contacts are frequently limited to virtual communication, making some remote workers feel detached and lonely. Human interaction is essential for emotional well-being, and when it is limited or absent, remote workers may experience increased emotions of loneliness, anxiety, or despair.

In addition to solitude, remote employment frequently results in blurred work-life boundaries.

While an office provides a clear physical barrier between professional and personal contexts, working from home might make it difficult to "switch off" from work. Many remote workers find themselves working longer hours without a clear finish to their workday. This blurring of boundaries can cause high stress levels and, over time, raise the risk of burnout. The absence of a clear workstation or routine frequently blurs the lines between work and relaxation, making it difficult for remote workers to maintain a healthy balance.

Furthermore, remote work can cause a lack of organization in everyday activities. Some employees find it difficult to develop a steady rhythm when there is no commute or traditional office routine. Without a consistent routine, it is easy to lose track of time, which can lead to increased worry and decreased productivity. For some, the lack of structure can have a negative influence on mental health by creating a sense of unpredictability, which can increase stress and reduce job satisfaction.

The Importance of Self-Care for Remote Workers

Self-care is crucial for everyone, but it is particularly important for remote workers who face unique stressors and obstacles. Including self-care routines in your daily routine can help prevent burnout, reduce stress, and promote general mental health. However, self-care is more than simply occasional pampering; it includes a variety of activities that nourish the mind, body, and spirit.

Physical self-care, for example, is crucial since it directly affects mental health. Regular exercise, a well-balanced diet, and adequate sleep all help to boost energy, attention, and mood. Even tiny amounts of physical activity, such as stretching or going for a short walk, can reduce stress and increase mental clarity, allowing remote workers to feel more connected and aware during the workday.

Emotional self-care is also essential for maintaining good mental health. This sort of self-care entails emotional management and processing, which is especially important for remote workers who frequently experience frustration, stress, or loneliness. Mindfulness activities, such as meditation or breathing exercises, can assist remote workers cope with stress and maintain emotional equilibrium. Recognizing and recognizing emotions, both positive and negative, is an effective method to deal with the difficulties of remote work. Journaling or talking to a therapist can be effective methods for processing emotions and sustaining emotional resilience.

Social self-care is another important aspect for remote workers because it entails developing relationships and making meaningful connections with others. While remote employment lowers in-person interaction, significant social relationships can still be maintained through virtual means. Regular check-ins with coworkers, virtual coffee breaks, and staying in touch with friends and family can help ease feelings of isolation. Participating in online communities or social groups can also create new connections and shared experiences, hence improving mental health.

Professional self-care is especially crucial for remote workers since it includes setting limits, successfully managing workloads, and taking required breaks. With the possibility of blurring barriers between personal and professional life, setting work hours and taking frequent breaks are critical steps toward avoiding burnout. Taking vacation and mental health days can give the relaxation you need to rejuvenate and maintain a healthy work-life balance.

Practical Strategies for Maintaining Mental Health

Maintaining mental health while working remotely necessitates deliberate techniques for stress management, boundary setting, and developing a balanced routine. Setting clear boundaries between work and personal life is one of the most effective ways to maintain mental health. Setting up a distinct workplace, having set work hours, and maintaining "off" times might help keep work from interfering with personal time. A specific workstation also signals to your brain that it is time to concentrate, and leaving that space at the end of the day helps to cement the separation between work and home life.

Developing a defined routine provides stability and predictability, which can lower stress and increase productivity. Creating a consistent morning routine that includes things like a nutritious breakfast, exercise, or mindfulness practice sets a good tone for the day. Scheduling work tasks in time blocks can help remote workers stay focused and efficient, whereas an end-of-day ritual, like as closing the computer or going for a brief walk, signals the change from work to personal time.

Maintaining relationships with coworkers, friends, and family is also important for mental wellness. Social interactions, especially virtual ones, can help remote workers avoid loneliness and stay focused. Staying socially engaged can be accomplished by scheduling virtual coffee breaks or informal discussions with colleagues, joining online networking groups, and planning regular check-ins with friends and family. These ties provide not just emotional support, but also a sense of community and camaraderie.

Taking regular breaks during the day is vital for maintaining mental health and productivity. According to research, taking brief, regular breaks can help you renew your mind and stay focused. Techniques such as the Pomodoro method, which involves working in intervals and taking brief breaks, can help remote workers manage their time more successfully. Step away from your desk for lunch or take a quick walk outside to relieve tension and boost vitality.

The Role of Employers in Supporting Mental Health

Employers have an important role in promoting the mental health of their remote workers. Companies may promote a culture of flexibility, open communication, and support, resulting in a healthier work environment for remote teams. Offering flexible work hours enables employees to manage personal and professional obligations, which is especially advantageous for remote workers who may be juggling caregiving or domestic duties.

Access to mental health resources, such as Employee Assistance Programs (EAPs), counseling services, or wellness initiatives, provides employees with the tools they need to manage stress and improve their overall well-being. Employers can also encourage mental health by encouraging employees to take regular breaks, mental health days, and vacation time, which helps them recharge and avoid burnout.

Employers should also take initiatives to promote connection and engagement among remote employees. Regular team meetings, virtual social events, and opportunities for collaboration all assist to lessen feelings of isolation and make remote workers feel like they're part of the team. A sense of community in the workplace is critical for employee engagement and motivation.

Mental health and self-care are critical for success in a remote working environment. Remote workers can preserve their mental health by dealing with issues such as isolation, fuzzy boundaries, and a lack of routine. Incorporating physical, emotional, social, and professional self-care into your daily routine is essential for stress management, burnout prevention, and maintaining a healthy work-life balance. Practical tactics such as setting limits, developing disciplined routines, and being socially connected allow remote workers to enjoy the flexibility of working from home without jeopardizing their mental health. Finally, emphasizing mental health enables remote workers to have a balanced, productive, and satisfying work experience, assuring long-term success and well-being in their remote employment.

# Staying Connected: Maintaining Relationships in Remote Work

One of the most difficult obstacles that remote workers confront is establishing meaningful relationships with colleagues, friends, and family. In typical office settings, social contacts occur spontaneously through casual talks, team meals, or simply being in the same physical place. However, in a remote work setting, these encounters are limited, and keeping engaged needs a concerted effort. Maintaining relationships is important not only for business success, but also for personal well-being. This chapter examines why keeping connected is critical and provides practical solutions for developing and maintaining meaningful relationships in a distant work environment.

**Why Staying Connected Matters**

Human connection is essential to our mental and emotional well-being. Maintaining relationships for remote workers entails more than just socializing; it also entails building a strong support network, encouraging cooperation, and remaining connected to the larger work community. Staying connected is vital for several reasons, including preventing isolation. Remote workers are more likely to feel lonely and alienated since they do not have regular, face-to-face interactions. Maintaining relationships combats loneliness, keeps us grounded, and reminds us of our role on the team.

Another reason to prioritize connection is to have a strong support network. A network of colleagues, friends, and family provides emotional and professional support in the form of feedback, guidance, and camaraderie. Strong relationships assist remote workers in overcoming problems, reducing stress, and promoting personal and professional development. Staying connected also promotes collaboration and teamwork. Regular communication and connection build a shared understanding and alignment among teams, increasing productivity and creativity. When team members are connected, it is easier to share ideas, collaborate, and achieve project objectives quickly.

## Strategies for Staying Connected with Colleagues

Maintaining professional ties over distance necessitates interactions that are not solely about work. Regular check-ins with coworkers can help foster a sense of belonging and keep everyone informed about work progress. These meetings do not have to be entirely official; often, informal chats deepen ties and foster a more unified work culture. Casual interactions throughout the week can help to bridge the physical barrier that separates people.

Participating in virtual social events is another great approach to remain in touch with coworkers. Many firms organize virtual team-building activities, such as online games or virtual happy hours. These activities provide an excellent opportunity to bond outside of work, fostering a collaborative and welcoming environment. Using collaboration platforms such as Slack, Zoom, or Microsoft Teams is also important for maintaining ties. These systems make it easy for remote teams to share ideas and debate projects, keeping them aligned and engaged. Remote work allows you to replicate virtual "water cooler" moments. Casual talks on messaging platforms are similar to spontaneous, non-work-related interactions that would normally occur in an office.

## Strategies for Staying Connected with Family and Friends

In addition to business contacts, distant workers must maintain personal connections. Working from home can blur the distinction between business and personal life, so it's critical to establish limits that safeguard personal time. Defining defined working hours and providing a specialized workstation assists remote workers to cognitively divide work and home life, leaving time for family and friends. Setting aside regular time to connect with loved ones is also crucial. Regular phone calls or virtual hangouts with friends and family provide a steady opportunity to keep connected, and in-person meetings, where possible, sustain those personal links.

Being truly present with family and friends is essential. Eliminating work-related distractions and focusing solely on loved ones improves the interaction. Turning off notifications during social events and setting away work devices allows remote workers to detach from work and reconnect with the people who are most important in their lives.

## How Technology Can Help You Stay Connected

Technology has become a vital tool for remote workers to keep connected to their professional and personal networks. Video conferencing platforms such as Zoom, Google Meet, and Microsoft Teams allow for face-to-face communication, which promotes personal connections and engagement. Video conversations offer a more meaningful contact than emails or chat messages, allowing distant workers to detect visual cues and emotions. Regular video check-ins with colleagues improve communication and bring a human element to the team dynamic.

Social media and messaging apps such as WhatsApp and Facebook Messenger make it simple to communicate with friends and family. These platforms enable casual, brief conversations that keep relationships alive. Joining online clubs or communities based on common interests can also create a sense of connection outside of one's immediate professional or familial circles, allowing remote workers to feel like they are part of a larger social network.

**Overcoming Challenges in Staying Connected**

It can be difficult to stay connected as a remote worker. Meetings can be challenging to schedule when teams are distributed across multiple time zones. Flexibility and understanding of others' schedules are critical for conquering this difficulty.

Using tools like World Time Buddy to establish mutually convenient hours or rotating meeting dates helps guarantee everyone has the opportunity.

Another typical barrier for remote workers is a lack of in-person engagement. While virtual contact can help bridge the gap, in-person events, team getaways, or coworking sessions—if possible—provide crucial opportunity for better interactions. Video calls, while not the same as in-person encounters, can contribute to a more personal and engaging experience than emails or chats alone.

Balancing work and social life can also be difficult in a remote work environment, as work and personal duties frequently overlap. Setting out time in your calendar for personal interests and social interactions is critical for preserving this balance. Techniques such as time-blocking allow remote workers devote time to both social contacts and professional responsibilities, resulting in a more balanced and pleasant remote work experience.

Maintaining relationships as a remote worker is critical to both personal well-being and professional success. Remote workers can stay connected with colleagues, friends, and family by engaging in intentional communication and using the correct technologies. Regular check-ins, participation in virtual social activities, and harnessing technology all help to foster relationships in a remote work environment. Despite the obstacles of remote work, prioritizing connection ensures that employees have a solid support network, feel less lonely, and may succeed both professionally and personally. The effort invested in building relationships makes remote employment more fulfilling, meaningful, and sustainable in the long run.

# Reviewing and Adjusting Your Routine

One of the most important aspects of a successful remote work lifestyle is having a daily routine that fosters productivity, balance, and well-being. In a traditional office setting, structure and external cues frequently dictate our habits. However, when working remotely, the person is solely responsible for developing an effective and lasting habit. However, no routine is flawless, and what works well at first may need to be tweaked later on. Regularly analyzing and updating your routine ensures that it remains effective, adapts to your changing needs, and supports your personal and professional objectives. This chapter will look at why it's important to examine your daily schedule on a regular basis, how to see indicators that it needs to be adjusted, and how to take practical steps to improve it.

## Why Regularly Reviewing Your Routine is Essential

Your daily routine is the cornerstone of how you handle both work and life, particularly when working remotely. Even the most well-planned routine might lose efficacy over time due to changes in living circumstances, workload, or personal priorities. Regular reviews enable you to uncover inefficiencies, avoid fatigue, and adjust to changing conditions, so making your routine durable and adaptive. For example, if duties alter, certain chores may no longer fit as easily into your schedule, and adapting to these changes can help you avoid dissatisfaction and stress. Reviewing your schedule also prevents rigidity, which can contribute to tiredness, and ensures that your daily activities are consistent with a healthy work-life balance. Keeping your routine fluid and adaptive improves your general well-being and allows you to stay connected with your goals.

## Signs That Your Routine Needs Adjusting

Certain symptoms suggest that it may be time to change your habit. Recognizing these signals early on will help you maintain productivity and a healthy work-life balance. One key indicator is a drop in productivity; if you realize that chores that used to flow effortlessly suddenly feel overwhelming or take longer to accomplish, it may indicate that your schedule has become inefficient. Another indicator is feeling frequently overloaded or burned out. A schedule that becomes excessively demanding or rigid can deplete your mental and physical energies, leaving you unmotivated and agitated. If you dread the start of each workday or are continually tired, it's a clear sign that you need a break or some changes.

Work-life balance is another common indication. Remote work frequently blurs the distinction between professional and personal life, causing some people to work late into the evenings or miss out on personal events. If you find yourself constantly sacrificing time for rest, family, or hobbies, it could indicate that your schedule needs to be rebalanced. Physical and mental tiredness are both crucial indicators. Long hours in front of a screen without enough pauses can cause headaches, back pain, eye strain, and mental fog. If you're having these problems, you might want to reconsider how much time you spend on uninterrupted work.

**Steps for Reviewing Your Routine**

It is not necessary to feel overwhelmed when evaluating your routine. You may utilize a few basic techniques to examine your schedule and make successful modifications. Start by tracking your time. Understanding how you currently spend your day gives you a clear picture of where time goes and reveals any inefficiencies. Over the course of one or two weeks, keep track of your activities, noting how much time you spend on work, personal activities, and breaks. Tools such as Toggl and RescueTime can provide precise insights into where you're most productive and where time may be slipping away.

Once you've gathered this information, examine it to uncover patterns and pain spots. Look for chores that routinely take longer than expected, times of day when your energy is low, or hobbies that create tension. These insights will identify areas for possible improvement. Prioritizing your activities is another important step in improving your routine. Not all tasks are equally important, and separating those that are critical from those that are less critical can save time and energy. Using the Eisenhower Matrix, for example, allows you to prioritize tasks based on urgency and importance, allowing you to focus on what is genuinely important.

Based on your findings, modify the time blocks for individual tasks. If you discover that particular activities routinely take more time than you have allotted, adjust your calendar to properly reflect these needs. Taking regular breaks is also important for avoiding burnout and staying focused throughout the day. Techniques such as time-blocking can help you organize time efficiently and ensure you have enough space for each task without feeling rushed.

**Practical Tips for Adjusting Your Routine**

After you've discovered areas for improvement, take tiny, attainable steps to make changes. Rather of redesigning your entire pattern, begin with a single component, such as your morning or evening plan. Testing minor modifications enables you to see what works without overwhelming yourself. Reassessing your goals is also beneficial, as your routine should be consistent with both your personal and professional aspirations. If your priorities have evolved, modifying your routine to reflect them will keep you on track to achieve your broader goals.

Rest and breaks are another essential component of a sustainable habit. Taking regular breaks helps to keep focus and avoid burnout. Consider using tactics like the Pomodoro Method, which entails working in 25-minute intervals with brief pauses, to efficiently regulate your energy levels. Testing and refining your routine is an ongoing process. As you implement changes, keep track of how they effect your productivity, energy, and equilibrium. Set recurrent reminders to assess your routine every few months to verify it is still satisfying your requirements.

**Adjusting to Life Changes**

As your life changes, so should your routine. Major life events such as relocation, new career duties, or family changes frequently necessitate more major adjustments. Maintaining a healthy lifestyle requires embracing flexibility and being willing to change your routine. Work-life integration is especially beneficial to distant workers. Given that personal and professional lives frequently cross in the home, developing a routine that incorporates both personal and professional tasks might help you stay focused and energized. Personal activities, such as exercise or family time, can be scheduled directly into your workday, resulting in a more harmonious balance.

Seasonal changes can have an impact on energy levels, workload, and personal responsibilities. For example, the end of the fiscal quarter may necessitate increased emphasis, whereas the summer months may allow for a looser schedule. Being aware of these changes and modifying your routine accordingly allows you to plan for both hectic moments and opportunities for relaxation.

Routine refining is a constant activity that keeps your professional and personal lives balanced and productive. You may create a routine that works for you in the short and long term by analyzing your schedule on a regular basis, recognizing inefficiencies, and making tiny, focused modifications. Tracking your time, prioritizing activities, and being flexible are all effective tactics for adapting to changes in your goals, workload, and personal commitments. The ultimate goal is to develop a routine that meets your changing demands, prevents burnout, and enables you to thrive both professionally and personally. A well-structured routine improves not only productivity but also overall quality of life, allowing remote workers to strike a satisfying and long-term work-life balance.

# CONCLUSION

Achieving and sustaining a healthy work-life balance in a remote workplace needs more than just time management; it necessitates a comprehensive strategy to nourishing both professional and personal well-being. The flexibility provided by remote work can considerably improve quality of life, but without structure, it can quickly lead to stress and imbalance. Setting clear boundaries, keeping a consistent routine, and maintaining a designated workstation will guarantee that your job and personal life receive the attention they need.

Self-care is also a major theme in this booklet. Without the discipline of commuting and in-person contacts, remote work can blur the distinction between professional and personal time, leading to burnout if not managed properly. Taking regular pauses, exercising your body, and engaging in activities that recharge you emotionally and physically are critical for maintaining your energy and well-being. Implementing tactics such as time-blocking, job prioritization, and allowing oneself to completely disengage after work hours will help prevent burnout and boost your overall success.

It's also vital to remember that work-life balance is a fluid and ever-changing process. As your personal life and job duties change, so will your approach to balance. Regularly examining your routines and boundaries allows you to adjust to these changes and ensures that work and life are in balance. Reflection journals, productivity monitors, and criticism from loved ones can all provide useful insights into how effectively you're balancing your responsibilities.

While much of this journey is personal, companies play an important role in creating a supportive work environment. Organizations that value flexibility, mental wellness, and respect for personal time foster an environment in which people may thrive. Consider using tools provided by your workplace, such as flexible hours, mental health days, or team-building activities, to improve your work-life balance. If such support is not accessible, take proactive in advocating for yourself by communicating openly about your requirements.

Finally, succeeding in a remote work environment requires striking a balance that feels right for you. There is no universal solution because everyone's situation and tastes are unique. However, by following the principles presented in this book setting boundaries, managing time thoughtfully, and prioritizing your well-being—you may achieve a satisfying and productive work-life balance. Remember that finding balance is a never-ending process of learning, changing, and evolving.

Here's to prospering in all aspects of life, achieving balance between work and personal life, and taking use of the unique perks that remote work provides!

www.ingramcontent.com/pod-product-compliance
Lightning Source LLC
Chambersburg PA
CBHW020636220526
45464CB00001B/177